WHAT NO ONE TELLS THE PASTOR'S WIFE

Gloria Lindsey Trotman

Special thanks for developmental funding
JUDITH A. THOMAS

Often pastors' wives are unprepared for the dynamics they encounter when they enter the ministry. On the surface and from distant observation, it seems as though the pastor's wife faces the normal, everyday challenges of any other professional woman. Onlookers consider her fortunate, especially since they perceive that beside her stands a man who's serious about his salvation and ready to deluge her with prayers. Ask any pastor's wife and she will uncover a few shocking revelations—not necessarily unpleasant, but staggering realities anyway. Why did someone not tell her about these things before? That is what this book is all about.

Many people helped me transform this book from a dream to reality:

Jim Cress, Ministerial Secretary of the General Conference of Seventh-day Adventists, who gave me constant encouragement, support, and affirmation.

Sharon Cress, Associate Ministerial Secretary and Shepherdess Coordinator of the General Conference of Seventh-day Adventists, my wonderful friend, whose unbelievable insight and sensitivity kept me going.

Peter J. Prime, Associate Ministerial Secretary of the General Conference of Seventh-day Adventists, whose confidence in my ability helped me believe in myself.

Israel Leito, President of the Inter-American Division of the General Conference of Seventh-day Adventists, whose unique, passionate interest in pastoral families and understanding shown to ministers' wives are unsurpassed.

Rae Lee Cooper, my friend, whose calm confidence and sincerity have impressed me over the years.

The several young pastors' wives who confessed common fears about their pastoral responsibilities, women who encouraged me to continue sharing material from my seminars, pastors' wives who willingly submitted their experiences for this publication.

Thank you, Shawna and Nelita, my second and third daughters, respectively, for your willingness to listen to sections of my draft from time to time and for your valuable input.

I owe much to our wonderful first-born daughter, Karen-Mae, for her sharp editorial skills and commitment to see me through this project.

My dear mother, who prepared me for the ministry of being a pastor's wife by the virtues she instilled in me.

And Jansen, my devoted husband, cheerleader, and the one who not only sensitized me to the many things a pastor's wife ought to know but also provided the title for this book.

Above all, I thank God for appointing me and instructing me to minister to our pastors' wives. His grace, mercy, and love have sustained me, and His blessings are innumerable.

To all pastors' wives—
present and future

Questions! We have questions. Not deep, theological imponderables—such may well be left to the theologians. Our questions are much simpler: Who? What? When? Where? How? Why?

Who sets the rules?

What are these rules?

When do they take effect?

Where are they written?

How can I ever know them?

Why didn't someone tell me?

Answers! Gloria Trotman has answers. Her new book, *What No One Tells the Pastor's Wife,* will share the answers with you.

Gloria, an experienced pastoral wife and a ministry leader herself, has written her new book for pastoral spouses and for prospective pastoral partners who have not yet even thought to ask many of the questions.

In these pages, you'll discover the rules—most of them unwritten but nevertheless strictly enforced—concerning the expectations for pastoral wives: marriage and ministry partner, lover, parent, manager, and (this one is really important) everything else the church members want you to do.

Gloria's words of wisdom will help you earn the rightful position of "first lady of your congregation." But before you rejoice in anticipation of such lofty status, remember what the members mean—you'll be the first lady they think to call when there's a problem to solve, a dinner to cook, a guest to host, a class to teach, or even a bathroom to clean.

You don't have to do all these things, but you should know that you'll be *expected* to accomplish all these things and more—and to do it with grace, poise, and polish, often with only 10 minutes' notice.

Why didn't anyone tell you? Why didn't someone prepare you? Well, now you'll know. And you'll be better prepared for the risks and rewards of being partners with the parson.

We urge every pastor, administrator, conference leader, local church elder, and board member to read and learn. You'll be learning from an expert! And when you comprehend the scope of the topic and revel in the plain answers and simple truths that Gloria shares, you'll really understand *What No One Tells the Pastor's Wife.*

James A. and Sharon M. Cress
Ministerial Association, General Conference of Seventh-day Adventists

TABLE OF CONTENTS

INTRODUCTION

I remember Week Two of our marriage as clearly as if it were yesterday. So much had happened. It all seemed to happen so fast. First, I was an ecstatic bride, then a shy wife. Soon I became a newcomer to another country, a nervous homemaker, and, of course, the pastor's wife. I recall being snatched from a "luxurious" two-day honeymoon and hurled into a series of evangelistic meetings. The fragrance of my bridal bouquet had hardly faded, and the taste of our wedding cake almost still lingered in my mouth. I was new, and I reveled in this feeling of "newness."

Then it happened! The honeymoon was literally over and exchanged places with reality. It was the first laundry day of Mr. and Mrs. Trotman. I could not believe my eyes as I sorted the unending pile of dirty laundry. *Where did all of these clothes come from*? Surely *"an enemy hath done this."* I cringed at the thought of hand-washing every piece of clothing. This new bride did not enjoy the luxury of a washing machine and dryer when she married the young ministerial intern. However, I was lucky to have a husband who helped me do the laundry. We called it our bonding experience. It really was not so bad after all. I was in for a new experience. No one had told me before that marriage would multiply the wash load! That laundry-day episode was only one of the things about which I was not forewarned. There were other experiences.

I had to face my first assignment of entertaining a senior minister. I studied and prepared for it as if I were facing an examination. The menu was simple, colorful, and nutritious. The table was correctly set. There was soft classical music in the background. The meal was ready. I must share here that the night before that special luncheon was a night of fitful sleep. So at least I needed to have an impressive meal to show for it.

All went well with the meal and the visiting pastor left our home, happy and well fed. I retreated to the kitchen to clean up, feeling very proud of myself. Then, to my horror, I discovered an item of the menu still sitting obediently, intact and untouched, in our oven! I learned two valuable lessons from that culinary experience: (1) Always make a list when planning to entertain, and (2) whatever can go wrong, will go wrong. Murphy's Law operates in the parsonage, too!

During our earlier months of marriage, I dutifully visited with my husband in the parish. There was a variety of reasons for the visits, which ranged from the praying for the sick and dying to encouraging the distressed or nurturing new members. When the cases were more complex or private, I did not accompany my husband. He went alone or with his Bible worker. I often evaluated my own motives for visiting with him. Was it because I liked meeting people or was it a requirement I was attempting to fulfill? Did I consider it an essential part of our team ministry? How much joy really swept through my soul as I ministered in this way? For several months these questions haunted me. However, there were two things about which I had no doubt. The dear church members usually expressed how happy they were to see me, and I was able to spend a few extra hours with my busy husband.

There were other occasions when reality mocked me. I had heard of curious eyes, but now I could feel them piercing my back. I had read of the pastoral fishbowl. Now I felt the chilly temperature as I waded around in its waters. No one had told me about that either.

The other day, a friend of mine shared an interesting experience with me. She revealed that after a few years in her pastoral marriage, she met the minister who had married them. She reminded him that they had not received premarital counseling, nor any survival tips for the ministry. "Why," asked my friend, "did you not tell me about some of the things a pastor's wife has to cope with?"

"Oh," replied the senior pastor glibly, "I did not want to spoil things for you."

Pastors' wives are not the only ones who need a sneak preview into marriage, the family, and career-related responsibilities. Life abounds in challenges, demands, disappointments, and pain for every wife. Life is also full of blessings, rewards, and miracles, smiles, hugs, and laughter.

Why doesn't someone tell us about these things in advance? Perhaps because most of us have also been taken by surprise. The truth? None of us have passed this way before. The good news? We are still passing this way, and we can share!

Gloria Lindsey Trotman

CHAPTER 1

MINISTRY MAY BE HAZARDOUS TO YOUR LIFE

For many of us, our earliest recollections of the lady who stood beside the pastor of our church were positive. She was "beautiful," which is the stock description of every pastor's wife. I can hardly recall an introduction of a pastor's wife that lacked that adjective. I still smile at a remark made by our third child after such an introduction of a visiting pastor's wife to our church one day. She demanded an explanation of me to her simple question: "Mommy, why do they say that all the time? Are all pastors' wives beautiful?"

We also noted that the pastor's wife smiled frequently, exhibited a quiet dignity, and partially concealed a percentage of her true self under a generous, broad-brimmed hat. Some wives occupied either the first or second pew and seemed to pay rapt attention to the proceedings, if their little pastoral brood permitted this. Other wives preferred to position themselves in the background or even attempted to remain *incognito*. My perception is that many of us at some time or another have wished for the ability to vanish when huge challenges confronted us. This is not a wish for permanent disappearance, just a yearning for a brief exit from view.

The other day a large sign greeted my eyes: BEWARE! HAZARDOUS SUBSTANCES. DO NOT COME WITHIN SIX FEET! I reflected on some of the hazardous substances that are constantly in the life of a pastoral family. Since it seems impossible to keep a safe distance from these, we find ourselves courting toxins as a way of life. Let us examine briefly some of these hazards.

Lack of Identity

One of our first challenges is to discover who we really are. Of course, every woman needs to find this out for herself. Pastoral families are often badgered by other people who seek to make them into what they are not or do not want to be. This is frustrating and sometimes painful. When we know ourselves and know what God expects of us, we do not easily become victims of this hazard. Knowing who we are and being comfortable with the revelation of ourselves is the first step toward maintaining our sanity. We will not be Play-Doh in the hands of our congregation or community. Instead we will be able to stand firm and confident, thereby enjoying a large measure of happiness.

How can we accomplish this? Sometimes we forget that God has given us the solution in His Word. We know our origin. We came from our Creator's loving hands. We also know whom we resemble. When someone tells us that we resemble a famous person, we feel a bit flattered. Who does not like to identify with fame and success? We know our origin. We were made in "His own image, in the image of God created he him; male and female created he them" (Gen. 1:27). We are unique objects of God's creation; even the hairs of our head are numbered (Matt. 10:30).

The picture gets better. I invite you to revel in this text with me: "Behold, I have graven thee upon the palms of my hands; thy walls are continually before me" (Isa. 49:16). My loving Father has me ever before Him. I am engraved in His palms. This is not a scratchy note. This is not an unintelligible scribble. This is an engraving in my Lord's palms. This represents a depth of our relationship, a permanent connection. I am thrilled to tears by this realization. But that is not all. Jesus died for me. So who am I? I am God's child and an object of His everlasting love. Now that I know who I am, I will not allow myself to be tortured by feelings of inferiority and the lack of identity.

Expectations

Dealing with expectations is another of the hazards of the pastor's wife. This can often place us in an uncomfortable situation. It sometimes seems as if we are drowning in a sea of expectations. There are the expectations from our spouses, from our friends, and from our children; most critical are the expectations from our congregations. These expectations seem to close in upon us and strangle us. I have discovered that expectations can be cruel and stifling. Little growth results from expectations. We experience more frustration and disappointment. Expectations can shackle and foster our lack of confidence when we perceive that we are not succeeding in meeting those expectations.

In an effort to deal with expectations, we find ourselves spinning in this direction and that direction. It is a dizzying exercise with futile results. I heard of a fisherman who was very proud of his fish and had visions of a lucrative market. Therefore, he decided to place a large sign outside his little hut. The sign read, "FRESH FISH SOLD HERE DAILY."

Along came a neighbor who thought the sign was too wordy. "Everybody knows that you will sell fresh fish. You will not want to advertise stale fish, would you?" said the neighbor. "Why not remove the word 'fresh.'"

So the vendor altered the sign to read, "Fish sold here daily."

The next day some of the fisherman's friends laughed at his sign. "Of course everybody knows that you are *selling* the fish. Take away the word 'Sold.' And as for that word 'here,' no one will think that your fish is sold anywhere else but here. So you do not need that word 'here.'

The fisherman changed the sign to read "Fish daily."

Soon after that, along came the fisherman's brother, who had just returned from college. "My dear brother, your sign is ambiguous. What do you really mean? Is there a river nearby where one can fish every day? I think not. What you *do* mean is that you sell fish here every day. Everybody knows that. You do not need the word 'daily.' "

So the fisherman removed the word "daily." All that was left was a solitary word—"Fish."

The next day a bright-eyed young man came upon the sign. "Fish?" he exclaimed, as he stared at the nebulous sign. "Fish what? Fish where?"

We cannot allow ourselves to dance to everyone's expectations. We have to process our talents and our convictions and let God's wisdom direct us.

Often people's expectations about our children are unrealistic and unfair. Are there not many of us who yearn to shelter our young from insensitive tongues and tactless remarks? Would somebody please accept that children will be children, even if they are the pastor's kids?

I thought I was prepared for the arrival of our first baby, Karen-Mae. I had read everything I could find about preparing for childbirth and the first years of our offspring. First, I discovered that childbirth was designed to remind me of the biblical account of the fall of man and the sentence of painful childbirth that was pronounced on the woman: "I will greatly multiply thy sorrow and thy conception; in sorrow thou shalt bring forth children" (Gen. 3:15).

Later I learned that tired, sleepy parents yielded their comfort to a yelling infant at two o'clock in the morning. I also found out that it was very easy to feel helpless and inadequate in the presence of a screaming, colicky baby. Amidst my futile efforts to comfort Baby Karen-Mae, I often dissolved into floods of tears. Somehow that made *me* feel better—not my baby. I am relieved that everyone in the world has only one "first-baby" experience in a lifetime.

I also discovered that I resented the curious stares of the "saints" at church while I attended to the pastoral baby. One day my baby was normal, fidgety, and peevish. She had cried a few times during the divine worship hour. Consequently I had had to make multiple trips outside of the sanctuary in order not to disturb the service. As I stood with my husband greeting the members and visitors after church, I overheard a dear sister telling my three-month old, "You have to remember that you are the pastor's child. You need to learn to behave." My head spun and my throat grew dry. A thousand "appropriate" retorts raced through my mind and competed for utterance; however, I held my peace. Why didn't someone tell me about all of these things before?

If our children are to emerge unscathed, we need to take time to understand their challenges. By involving them in creative witnessing, we can help them find joy in serving Jesus. Also we need to shield them from the problems of the ministry. Find ways for them to have fun and to enjoy their childhood. Build happy memories of the time spent as a family.

By training our children to be Christians and by affirming them regularly, we can help our kids to survive the torrents of expectations. They need our prayers. Pray for a "hedge of protection" around them. Make time for them. Shower them with unconditional love.

Financial Stress

Many references are made to the importance of gymnastic ability for financial maneuvers in the pastoral family. Now I had to take an intensive in money management. This in-service training had to be quick and successful; there was no margin for error. A pastor's wife has to be a financial magician. She has to work miracles with dollars—dress herself and her family well, look well, feed the parishioners well, be a benefactor, and pray frantically to the Lord to keep her afloat.

Every Christian needs to practice money management. It may be necessary to attend financial management seminars or even visit a financial counselor to get help. As Christian stewards we need to pay attention to the handling of our finances. There are many ways our families can unite to cut costs. We can conserve on the use of water and electricity. The use of coupons and special sales purchases can aid any wife in stretching the dollar.

It is true that the pastor's salary does not often equal that of other professionals with similar academic qualifications. Yet he is expected to maintain certain lifestyle characteristics of an ambassador for Christ. Through this there are a couple pitfalls that the pastoral couple must shun. We ought not cry to our parishioners for financial help. Borrowing from members of our congregation is unacceptable.

Oh, but we have a loving Savior who never stops providing for us. When we give God His part of our income, He blesses the remainder of our money. I have experienced many dollar-stretching miracles and constant reminders that God is able to take care of our needs even before we ask Him.

Over-commitment

"I am so tired all the time. I just do not seem to be able to meet all of my appointments." This was the comment of a young pastor's wife.

I asked her what her program was like. It was a whirlwind of responsibilities. She had been in charge of the children's division at her church. She was the church pianist as well as one of the directors of the children's choir. She was also an accountant at a large firm. Of course she had three young children, and her husband pastored a large church. This young woman was on a sure path to burnout or even a break-down. She needed to evaluate her program and focus on her priorities.

Sometimes feelings of guilt force a pastor's wife to over-commit herself. This is not the desire of our Father. There are times in a woman's life when she may not be able to be as active in church as she would like to be. It is difficult for a pastor's wife with toddlers or a baby and very young children to serve in as many capacities as a woman whose children are older and less dependent on her. We are being unfair to ourselves and our families when we allow parishioners to determine our workload. We know the size of our plates as well as our physical and mental capacities. Therefore, we need to pick areas in which to serve that will not sacrifice our families and our own health.

Let us note the wise words of Dorothy Kelley Patterson in her book, *A Handbook for Ministers' Wives:*

"As a minister's wife, to attempt to mold your life into meeting the expectations of your parishioners will send you to disaster and disillusionment on the fast track. You aren't meant to busy yourself dancing for the pipers . . . rather, your task is genuine and sincere commitment to the responsibilities God has given you. The rest of the script will unfold according to God's plan for you." (5)

Let us trust God to direct us in the areas of service and also to give us the wisdom to prioritize.

Emotional Overload

As pastoral couples we are deluged with the problems of our church members. Multiple counseling sessions and committees, board meetings, funerals, terminal illnesses of a church member or two, in addition to our own challenges, can drain our emotional resources. To internalize the stresses and strains of our parish comes very easily. Although difficult, but necessary, we should lay aside these problems in order to revitalize our energies to continue our service to humanity. The young mother who has experienced a miscarriage, the teenager who was discovered to be on drugs, the pregnant teen, the abusive family, the couple with fertility challenges, the father who has lost his job—these are events that overload the pastoral couple emotionally. Here is where an exercise program, a vacation, or just resolving to take a break from these problems will help greatly. Watch a funny movie or get a massage. We must find ways to throw off the cloak of care-giving for a while in order to restore our strength to serve.

Coping Strategies

How do we deal with the hazards of ministry? There is an increase in the number of pastors' wives who are candidates for depression with a combination of factors that leads to this condition. The burden of the pastorate is a major contributing factor. Women who feel overwhelmed, sad, tearful, or weak need to see a doctor. If one prefers to withdraw from company most of the time, loses an interest in her grooming, or becomes absent minded, a visit to the doctor is recommended. Sometimes what others consider insignificant or trivial may loom as a large, threatening factor in the eyes of this woman. This is the time to see a physician. We women must take care of our health.

It is a good idea to identify one's stressors. What is causing nervousness, the tightening of the stomach muscles, or anxiety? Are problems or people draining us of our strength? There must be a method of releasing ourselves from these weights. Put the problems on the back burner. Go out with a friend or two, and find something to laugh about.

Finally, by increasing your intimacy with God, you will experience a renewed look at your ministry. Spend quiet moments with Him. Engage in regular prayer sessions with your spouse. Also, praise God often. I like the recommendation of the psalmist, "Seven times a day will I praise Thee" (Ps. 119:164). This means that we, like the psalmist, should be praising God throughout the day. Praise drives the agents of hell and darkness away.

Perhaps no one told the new pastor's wife about the professional hazards. However we can be assured of the promise in God's Word: "Being confident of this very thing, that he which hath begun a good work in you will perform it until the day of Jesus" (Phil. 1:6).

CHAPTER 2

WHO IS THIS STRANGE MAN I MARRIED?

"I now pronounce you man and wife." How many pastoral brides really hear and understand this pronouncement of the marriage officer? The new husband is a man. He is a God-created male with all the attendant rights, privileges, and idiosyncrasies that "appertain thereto." Someone has said that after every wedding comes a marriage. Into this marriage enter a man and a woman. The participants in a pastoral marriage are first a man and woman, then a pastor and his wife. "So God created man in his own image, in the image of God he created him; male and female he created them" (Gen. 1:27, NIV). This text applies also to pastoral couples. So God created "male and female," not the pastor and his wife.

Unless we allow ourselves to come in touch with who we are from creation, we move around in a plastic chamber filled with figurines and reflections. This robs us of the ability to deal with the reality of life. On one hand, our husbands must realize that we are women with female behaviors, needs, and sensitivities. On the other hand, we wives need to admit to our husbands' "maleness"—their clinical perceptions, their strengths, and their vulnerabilities.

Men and women often face challenges in understanding each other. Much friction in marriage could be eliminated if the genders understood each other better. Greater marital harmony would be enjoyed if husband and wife exerted a willingness and effort to study each other.

Physical Differences

One of the physical differences between males and females is in the area of strength. Generally, men have more muscle and more physical strength. However, women tend to live longer than men. The skin of women is usually smoother, while the skin of most men is tougher. Although women boast survival of the excruciating pain of childbirth, there has been the controversial verdict that men have a higher pain threshold. In other words, while women scream and even faint in the face of severe pain, men are able to cope better in similar situations. We are still wondering if male pride is a strong supporting factor of male survival of severe pain.

Mental and Emotional Differences

The line of demarcation between the mental capacities of men and women seems to be getting fainter. Generally, women have better verbal ability, but men tend to excel in spatial ability. We notice, though, that more women are displaying improved spatial performance, and men are also excelling in verbal areas. In fact, while women generally have more acute verbal ability, more men are instructors in languages. In general, women talk more than men. When men talk, they are more concise in their approach, thereby using about half as many words as women.

The emotional differences are marked. Women are intuitive, feeling, and expressive. We are also a puzzle to our men in the way we express our emotions. We cry when we are happy and shed pools of tears when we are sad. My husband has been urging me to choose the occasions when I want to cry or dance. I weep at weddings, graduations, and funerals. I cry at departures and reunions. Beauty of music or art blinds me with tears. What a bundle of contradictions we women are!

Men are factual, clinical, and generally far less expressive. This is difficult for us women to understand. Women are very sensitive about their bodies and their professional accomplishments. They crave affirmation and are prone to suffer from low self-esteem. Husbands should note this. Although men often present a more confident appearance, they do have fragile egos. Wives ought to be aware of this and avoid fracturing their spouses' egos.

Differences in the Approach to Romance

Romance and expressions of love are an integral part of a woman's make-up. Men are sometimes too busy or too factual to be romantic. Perhaps it is not such a bad idea that stores bombard us with Valentine's Day reminders. A few years ago a young man remarked to me that he had recently bought a new family car; therefore, his young wife had better not expect anything for Valentine's

Day. "I mean, not even a card," he clarified.

This comment stunned me. I feared that he had missed the point completely. What did the purchase of a car two months before have to do with a Valentine's Day card? This man was certain that by buying a new car, he was demonstrating his love. I knew better. I felt that in the heart of a woman, a simple card expressing his love would be of "more value than many" cars. So I dared to suggest that he buy his wife a little card. In fact, I said that it would be a good idea to buy her a card for no special reason or special day as a rule.

A few months after that meeting, I met the young husband. "Do you remember," he volunteered, "that little conversation we had about Valentine's Day? Well, you should have seen how happy my wife was when she received the roses I took her."

"Oh, I am so proud of you," I responded. I felt very happy for his wife.

That is how it is with us women. We are sentimental. We are avowed romantics. Flowers, candlelight, and chocolates will continue to be significant to a woman. Frequent protestations of love will always be welcome to the female ear. We women will continue to be unforgiving of a spouse who forgets our birthdays and anniversaries. We also like to be held, hugged, cuddled, and kissed. A woman is a romantic creature.

Her Expectations

Sometimes a pastor's wife tends to forget that she is married to a *man*. Her being married to a pastor is ever in her thoughts. This perception can spell disappointment and sometimes even disaster as she demotes herself from the position of partner to parishioner. This means that she shackles herself with the typical expectations of a church member. Her objectivity is reduced because of her tendency to view her spouse with the typical godlike regard of some church members. This also means that her husband can do no wrong. How then can a wife be of help to her husband? Also, her confidence as an equal partner is threatened. Did anyone tell the pastor's wife that she is married, first of all, to a man?

The expectations that a pastor's wife has of her husband are basically the same as those of any non-pastoral wife. She expects that her physical, social, and economic needs will be attended to. In addition to that, however, she longs to have her spiritual needs met. When the pastor's wife presents her problems to her husband, she expects a "let us pray" response. This is not likely to happen as often as she had dreamed. The spouse is more likely to volunteer a quick solution, discuss the problem with her in a concise fashion, trivialize it, or perhaps merely suggest that *she* pray about it—by herself! This is disappointing to her because pastors are *supposed* to pray with people who have problems, even if those people are their wives. They do pray with and for the parishioners, don't they? Why should it be different where the wife is concerned? A number of pastors' wives have wondered about this.

His Needs

The expectations that the pastor has of his wife are generally similar to what any other male has of his spouse. Men often complain that their wives do not understand them. These men contend that greater spousal understanding would foster better marital satisfaction. Since men usually prefer to suffer in silence, they rarely verbalize their feelings. When was the last time you heard a man complain, "I am not being appreciated around here!" Possibly never. However, if a woman feels neglected or under-appreciated, we would hear about it in clear, fluent tones, but men do like to feel loved and appreciated. It is a good thing for us to tell them that they are special to us.

A man needs to have his ego constantly rebuilt or kept intact. Spouses who are ego builders are appreciated by their husbands. A variety of things can wound a man's ego. Minimizing the importance of his job or his role as provider is one way of hurting his ego. Men like wives who understand how important their jobs are to them. When people underestimate a man's ability and humiliate him especially in public, he is devastated. Men like respect, as well as being made to feel important and competent.

Men like wives who take care of their homes. Keeping a home comfortable, clean, and beautiful is a major challenge for wives, especially for those who work outside of the home. Add to this a couple of younger children and the dream can easily become a nightmare. However, everyone likes coming home to an inviting house. Wives need to find shortcuts and ways to help them in their housework. It is a good idea to encourage a husband to help in the home. Children should also be taught to assist by doing age-appropriate tasks. Schedules and lists can help to organize domestic tasks and relieve the strain on the homemaker.

Men also need the emotional and spiritual support of their wives. They like us to listen to them when they venture to speak out. A wise wife will embrace that rare opportunity. Do not hesitate to let your husband know that you are praying for him. Offer to pray with him too. There is untold power in prayer.

Discuss your goals with your husband. Affirm his successes and commit to being his support. At the same time, try to discover your own talents and enjoy the confidence of your own abilities. Promise yourself to complement your husband rather than compete with him. Remind him often that you are happy to be his wife. That is what marital partnership is all about.

Be careful with your moodiness, nagging, and constant criticism. Men hate these. Even King Solomon could not tolerate this. He expresses a strong preference for living in the corner of a housetop or even in the wilderness rather than dwelling in a mansion with a brawling, contentious, or angry woman (Prov. 19:13; 21:9, 19; 25:24). He seems to have had his share of nagging, because he states in clear terms, "A continual dropping in a very rainy day and a contentious woman are alike" (Prov. 27:15). King Solomon is clearly an expert on these behaviors of women. With 1,000 women in his life at once, how could he be less informed? (1 Kings 11:1-3).

The mother or wife sets the tone for the home. What a responsibility! Heavy workloads, financial demands, and insufficient rest contribute to flaring tempers and unpleasantness. How then can a woman keep her sweetness and an even temper? Commit your workload to the Lord. Ask God to give you His peace and the comfort of the Holy Spirit. It works!

We cannot fail to mention that a man likes a wife he can trust. Men do not express their feelings easily, and when they do, women need to be understanding and confidential. If a wife behaves like a newscaster and exposes her husband's feelings to others, he will clam up and never confide in her again. We need to regard our husbands' hopes, fears, and dreams as sacred.

We must not overlook the sexual needs of men. In *His Needs, Her Needs,* Willard Harley records the results of a study he conducted among some male and female subjects regarding their hierarchy of needs. The results were astounding. Let us take a look at how the men ranked their top five needs in descending order of importance:

1. Sexual satisfaction
2. Recreational companionship
3. An attractive wife
4. Domestic support
5. Admiration

The women in the survey had different priorities. Observe their top five needs:

1. Affection
2. Conversation
3. Honesty and frankness
4. Financial support
5. Commitment/responsibility to family. (182 – 184)

We cannot help noticing that while sexual satisfaction is at the top of the five most critical needs of the males, it does not appear on the list of the top five needs for women in this study. Perhaps here is a good place to remind ourselves that pastors are males, too.

In the beginning God made us different, "male and female created he them" (Gen. 1:27). It is necessary to understand our differences and our gender-specific needs. Our gender differences influence our needs. An understanding of gender needs leads to tolerance, patience, peace of mind, and marital harmony.

It is futile and frustrating to try to change each other. Let change begin with us. We need the courage to examine ourselves to see what kinds of persons we are. Ask God to give you a spirit of introspection. Like the psalmist, let our prayer be, "Search me, O God, and know my heart: try me and know my thoughts: and see if there be any wicked way in me, and lead me in the way everlasting" (Ps. 139:23, 24). Then let us be willing to accept and appreciate our differences. Let each wife celebrate the uniqueness of the man she married.

Here is a list my husband and I compiled some time ago based on responses from participants in our seminars:

WHAT HUSBANDS WANT THEIR WIVES TO KNOW ABOUT MEN

1. They need their wives to be their ego-builders.
2. They need to feel loved, appreciated, and accepted.
3. They need to feel important, competent, and worthwhile.
4. They need to feel that they are in charge of their homes.
5. They need wives that complement them, not compete with them.
6. They need wives who are proud of their femininity.
7. They need wives who keep themselves desirable and attractive.
8. They need wives who take care of their homes.
9. They need wives who understand that their husbands' jobs are important to them.
10. They need wives who fulfill their husbands' sexual needs.
11. They need emotional and spiritual support from their wives.
12. They need wives who make an effort to harness their moods.
13. They need wives they can trust.
14. They need wives who respect them and make them feel special.
15. They need wives who are happy to be married to them.

CHAPTER 3

LONELY DAYS, LONG NIGHTS

A new pastor's wife in search of empathy complained to the wife of a senior pastor that she was feeling lonely.

"Lonely! Why should a child of God be lonely? I am not one of those who feel lonely. I guess I have too many things to do, and besides I have a wonderful Friend, Jesus," declared Sister I-Have-It-All-Together.

I hardly think these remarks were of much help to the young minister's wife. Let us not be too hard on this dear sister, though. Perhaps the older lady really did not experience feelings of loneliness. Perhaps her earlier days of ministry were so far in the historical past that she could no longer recall such feelings. Perhaps she was not the type of person to pamper herself with friends and the attention of others. She could very well have been one of those people who adore solitude and is not affected by not having companionship. For whatever reason, she and loneliness were not partners. There are not many women like her, though.

Another pastor's wife tried to explain to her husband that she missed him greatly when he was out of town. He refused to even try to understand her feelings. He was very defensive and even insensitive. His reply was, "What do you expect me to do? Do you want me to do my job from our house?" His attitude seemed to suggest that this poor woman was an unreasonable, complaining, uncooperative wife who was totally unmindful of her husband's "call to service." If only he had been patient and caring enough to listen to his wife's cry and tried to work things through with her, the woman would not have experienced the pain she did. What this pastor did not realize was that he was driving his spouse to abhor the ministry. Sometimes all a woman needs is to be listened to. In the pastorate, this can be a luxury.

Many ministerial wives complain of loneliness. They are not necessarily great party-lovers, nor do they claim to need round-the-clock excitement or attention. But they do experience loneliness. One wonders how this is possible when pastoral wives are so often in the center of the action. A long time ago, King David also experienced loneliness. His loneliness hurled him into a state of insomnia. "I lie awake, and am like a sparrow alone on the housetop" (Ps. 102:7). What vivid imagery! Yet this describes the plight of many pastors' wives. We are in full, elevated view of a world of people, and yet we are lonely.

There are some definite reasons for loneliness. Moving to a new location is a common cause. Most people resent moves. The pastor's wife spends her life moving from one place to another. Sometimes, before she is able to cement relationships in one parish, along comes another mandate to move. There is the other side of the coin. The pastoral family may have established solid friendships that are threatened by a transfer to another parish. Some people are slower than others in making new acquaintances. If the pastor's wife is not a gifted social mixer but likes relationships anyway, her new life could be tinged with loneliness.

Traveling husbands can also be a contributing factor to loneliness in the life of a pastor's wife. Many wives have expressed their dread of having husbands who travel extensively. Some of these spouses do not enjoy sound sleep when their husbands travel. Others are scared, and others just cannot settle into a normal routine when the pastor is away. I am able to empathize with these wives because I remember my earlier days of having a traveling husband. For some unexplainable reason, sleep eluded me, and when I did manage to fall into a fitful sleep, it was just a few hours before dawn! Then one day, the Lord showed me two texts:

"I will both lay me down in peace, and sleep; for thou, Lord, only makest me dwell in safety" (Ps. 4:8). "I laid me down and slept; I awaked; for the Lord sustained me" (Ps. 3:5). Those texts were the solution to my insomnia. Night after night, I felt ensconced in the arms of my loving Lord, and I slept like a baby for a number of nights. Whenever difficulty in sleeping returned, I clung to those texts.

When Everything Seems To Go Wrong
Have you ever noticed that when our husbands are away, all kinds of events seem to creep into our lives to scare, frustrate, or confuse us? The other day

I made a list of things that often go wrong when the pastor-husband is on a trip:

1. One or two kids get the flu.
2. The dog urgently needs to go to the vet.
3. The plumbing needs fixing.
4. The washing machine breaks down.
5. The school principal needs to see us immediately.
6. Our child gets appendicitis.
7. There is car trouble.
8. The babysitter quits.
9. The telephone won't work.
10. A dangerous hurricane comes to town.
11. There are a few burglaries in the neighborhood.
12. We get locked out of the house by accident.

Of course there are many other items that may be added to this list. One pastor's wife asked me a few months ago, "Why is it that a normal, uneventful household turns into a center of excitement, chaos, and near-disaster when the pastor leaves town?"

I had no answer. I have always asked myself that question. *Why does everything seem to flow smoothly when Jansen is at home, and the moment he leaves, the tempo changes from an even rhythm to a wild, syncopated beat?* I know one thing, though. These experiences have increased my dependence on God. I can always say that through it all, my heavenly Father watches over me.

Lack of adult companionship can also lead to loneliness. If a mom has a brood of preschoolers as her only companions, she could easily long for someone of a more mature age with whom to share her thoughts. Imagine having to limit one's conversation to responding to requests for peanut-butter-and-jelly sandwiches or to "Mommy, please tell Timmy to stop hitting me" or the common toddler's demand of "Tory, weed tory, Mommie. Tory, tory peese." Then Mom has to find the kid's favorite book and read for the umpteenth time that special story. This is Mom's daily routine. Then when at last the exhausted adult spouse returns home from his pastoral rounds, it is often too late to have a meaningful conversation.

"Well, how about making some friends?" someone suggests. Good idea! Often shyness deprives us of the precious experience of friendship. God made a world full of people. There must be somebody out there who can be a friend to us. We need only to be brave enough to initiate a friendship. This is an excellent cure for loneliness.

Here are some ways to beat loneliness:

1. Try to find ways to stay busy. Choose a project and work on it. Give yourself a realistic deadline. The sense of fulfillment that follows is immeasurable.

2. Do something for somebody. Turning the focus away from ourselves is a wonderful deterrent for loneliness.

3. Develop a skill. There is always room for self-improvement.

4. Discuss your feelings of loneliness with your spouse. Do not complain, but share your feelings with him. Let him know that you understand the demands of his job. You are not asking him to neglect his responsibilities, but you want him to know how much you miss him when he is away. You may want to tell him that it is really important to you that he at least acknowledge that you are the best judge of your own feelings. Ask him to give you some suggestions to help you overcome your loneliness.

5. Make some friends. Allow people to catch a glimpse of your friendliness. There are some people in your congregation to whom you can become a precious friend. The sick, elderly, and shut-in need your friendship. They will value a visit from you.

6. Work on yet another project. You may want to do some redecorating or sewing. Try out a new recipe. Learn a new song. Plant a garden.

7. Do not be intimidated by people. Be confident as you interact with them.

8. Develop an attitude of praise. The spirit of praise puts a sparkle in your eyes and a glow on your face. You will become magnetic.

9. Learn to appreciate and enjoy your own company.

10. Talk to God about your loneliness. He created you to be a social being. Repeat several of His precious promises. They will fill you with strength and hope.

We need to differentiate between loneliness and solitude. Loneliness is painful and sometimes spawned by our own attitudes. Loneliness can lead to self-pity and personal discomfort. Solitude is a gift that can be of great benefit to us. Through solitude we can find out who we are. Through solitude we can connect with God. Through solitude we are refreshed and renewed to improve our own lives and to serve others. The good news is that loneliness is not incurable! The sensational news is that you are not alone, for God always honors His promise to "never leave you nor forsake you" (Josh. 1:5).

CHAPTER 4

YOU NEED TO BE A STUNT WOMAN?

Most of us have sat transfixed as we watched skilled movie stars perform hair-raising stunts. We wondered how these actors could be so multi-talented. A dashing young man would jump several feet off a building onto a moving car. A dainty non-athletic looking female would somersault several times in the air, twisting and turning, then splash into a pool. They hypnotized us in front of the television screen. It took maturity and experience or even a tour around Hollywood for us to realize the existence and role of stunt men and women.

Stunt men and women form an important part of many movie productions. Sometimes nearly 50 percent of the actors in a movie are stunt specialists. One part of a film may begin with the movie star attempting a jump. The cameras will be stopped for a short while, and then a stunt man will be photographed doing the major role of jumping. After the cameras are stopped again, the actor will resume the jump just a few safe feet from the ground, so that his face may be seen on the screen. Sometimes dummies are used for the more dangerous, unbelievable feats. Viewers are awed by the "acrobatic ability" of movie actors.

The pastor's wife is often considered a stunt woman. Alice J. Taylor puts it this way: "So much is expected of her—the health of an Amazon and dedication of a Florence Nightingale; the patience of Job and the zeal of a Carrie Nation; the peace-loving thoughts of a Ghandi and the fighting spirit of a warrior; the charm of a debutante and the intelligence of a Phi Beta Kappa. Besides this, she must live her life in a goldfish bowl, well aware that it is her sole responsibility to see that the goldfish behave." (14)

The Scholar of Theology
The telephone rang for the ninety-ninth time that morning. I answered

quickly and professionally, hoping the caller would sense the urgency in my voice and spare me too many details. It was almost noon, and preparation of the lunch had not even been a thought. What a morning it had been! I was balancing my time between multiple calls and taking care of Child #3, a three-month old newcomer. Finally I had been able to put the baby down for a mini nap. I had plans for that very short grace period.

"Hello," responded the caller. "Is the pastor at home?"

"I am sorry, he is not. Who may I tell him is calling, and may I take a message, please?"

"Well, I have a Bible question for him, but as the pastor's wife, you ought to know the answer. You see, our little Bible study group was discussing this text, and we needed some guidance."

"Well, that's nice." I replied, trying to sound less hurried. "I am quite ready to write the text and your number, and I will be sure to pass on your message to my husband as soon as he returns home."

"Well," continued the voice on the other end of the line, "I was hoping that you could help me."

"I will not be able to help you as much as the pastor can. I would be happy to attempt it, but now is not a good time. You see, the baby—"

"I thought pastors' wives knew their Bibles," was the caustic comment.

Uh-oh, I guess this stunt woman was a bitter theological disappointment to her parishioner!

There are times when pastors' wives can give sensible answers to Bible questions. We do study our Bibles and can generally comment intelligently. Every Christian woman should immerse herself in the study of God's Word. We pastors' wives do not claim to be as skilled as our husbands, and that is all right too, since we do not have a monopoly on knowledge. When we do not know, we need not feel like underachievers. One should not be embarrassed to admit her lack of understanding on some topics and be willing to research a subject. We should be willing to keep on learning.

The Five-Talent Woman

We are expected not only to *know* everything but also to be able to *do* everything. Perhaps this makes us candidates for some kind of award? We have to organize banquets, plan weddings, produce programs, teach Bible classes, play the church piano or organ, and prepare meals for the crew working on a clean-up day. Best of all should be our ability to fill any gaps in the program of the church. Add to this list an immaculate house and 'round-the-clock' service to parishioners. Is there a woman on this planet who could fill this list of dizzying demands?

We must not allow ourselves to be frustrated by these expectations. It is not necessary to have five talents. We know our talents and limitations, and we must balance our priorities. It is fair to believe that as first ladies of the church, we should be knowledgeable about the major areas of social living. We ought to study the rules of etiquette and standards for entertaining. We need to have a refined taste in dress, in speech, and in the practice of appropriate behaviors. We will not know everything there is to know, but by reading and attending seminars and by exposing ourselves to correct social behaviors, our confidence and competencies will increase. By improving ourselves as leaders, we will also be able to teach others.

The Mind Reader

Have you ever met someone who was upset with you for reasons unknown to you? I have. This is quite a delicate situation. You may have allegedly said something the person did not like, and of course you had no idea of that. The person was angry and kept on being angry with you because you did not apologize. You did not apologize because you were unaware of the damage you caused. So you are met by a cold, somber face, and that is your clue that something is the matter.

Perhaps you did not see someone while you were driving along a busy street or while you were sprinting through the aisles of the supermarket. You might even have looked in the person's direction but not seen them. That is a major offense. That person harbors the hurt, and you are supposed to know about it. Mind reader? How sad.

Really, we cannot do much about ultra-sensitive people, and we must not permit them to make our lives miserable. We will encounter difficult people from time to time. The apostle Paul prepared us for this: "If it be possible, as much as lieth in you, live peaceably with all men" (Rom. 12:18). Living in peace "'with all men" may not always be possible. Some people revel in discord and disunity. They may even confront us in anger. However, we must not match their difficult behavior. We may not be able to change their thoughts toward us; however, we can conduct ourselves in a respectable fashion and demand that we be treated with respect. We dare not allow ourselves to be caught up in the other person's moodiness or angry outbursts. We must try to stay calm and above the situation. It may be necessary to politely remove ourselves from the flammable scene when we sense that the situation is getting out of control. Then forget about the confrontation, forgive, and move on. "And be ye kind one to another, tenderhearted, forgiving one another, even as God for Christ's sake hath forgiven you" (Eph. 4:32).

Time: Friend or Foe?

The other day one of my friends said that she wished there were about 40 hours in a day. *Why would she want to cram a week's work into one day?* I felt sorry for her. I wondered if she really liked working that much. Well, people are different. Some of us wish we had more time to get our work done. Others faithfully deduct seven hours for sleep and then hope that there will be enough time for them to accomplish their tasks. Then there are a few "haunted" mortals who feel that it is immoral to rest or relax. Many of us do not have the luxury of extra time. What can we do to prevent time from becoming an enemy?

There are many books and seminars available on time management. As pastors' wives, we sometimes get into trouble with our husbands when we contribute to their lateness for appointments. Actually, we do not have to cause our husbands to be tardy. It is all about making a commitment to be on time. I have been able to survive multiple engagements with an "A" in punctuality. My husband has never been able to accuse me of making him late. Here are a few success secrets:

1. Start early. Find out the time of the appointment as well as the projected departure time. Count backward so that you have an accurate idea of when you ought to start getting ready. You may need two or more hours to get ready for event, or perhaps you may not need so much time. The more formal the occasion, the more time is needed for preparation. Plan ahead on what you are going to wear. That usually

takes longer than actually getting dressed.

2. Communicate with your spouse about your expectations when you are going out together. You may need him to help you get the children ready if they are young. It is better to let him know that there are certain magical feats you need help with so that you both can go to the event in pleasant spirits. Often the poor wife has to do multiple chores all by herself and still get the family all ready to leave on time. This makes her disgruntled and feeling sorry for herself. Here is where communication is of extreme importance. Delegate responsibility. Some women are expected to prepare the meals, feed the kids and husband, clean up the kitchen, and get the family ready to go. This is very stressful. Decide what has to be done before you leave and what will have to remain for later. It is also a good idea to let Hubby know that you would appreciate advance notice when you are going out together. This will help you in your planning.

3. Being on time is most challenging when we have babies and toddlers. There are some things we can do ahead of time, however. Always have the baby's bag packed. Upon returning home from an appointment, promptly remove soiled clothes and bits of trash. Replenish diapers and have the bag ready with everything (except formula) for the next trip. Keep a bag of crayons, coloring books, toys, and an extra change of clothing always ready so that you will avoid the last-minute dash to pack these.

4. Make a commitment that you and your husband will earn the reputation of being punctual. This is expected of professionals. People lose respect for those who do not value other people's time. Christ's ambassadors should be no less responsible in the use of His time.

Now what about time for yourself? Many ladies complain that they do not have the luxury of time for themselves. This is true sometimes and very sad. Trying to eek out some time for oneself is a feat when a mother has younger children. Women often say, "I cannot afford that kind of time." I say, "You cannot afford *not to* find that kind of time." Time for ourselves is so important that we have to plan for it. This may sound idealistic, but try making the effort and see how things work out. Start by aiming at tiny bites of time. You may be able to set aside a bit of time at the beginning of the day. A devotional period, even if it is just a few minutes, will help you start the day right. Or perhaps you may choose to take some personal time late at night.

It can be frustrating to plan to have time for yourself at the beginning of the day, before the kids wake up, and then the baby awakes 20 minutes ahead of schedule. The point is that many things contrive to rob us of time for ourselves. At least we can make a plan. If you work outside of the home, perhaps you can snatch a bit of your lunch break to do something for yourself. You may not need a whole hour to eat lunch. Then perhaps you could spend 15 minutes reading that book you love. Stay-at-home moms have a greater challenge in assigning time for themselves, especially if they have babies or toddlers.

Start with a to-do list. At night before going to bed, make a list of things you have to do. Do not make a crowded list for one day; leave some vacant slots. One of those slots could be time for you. Take a look at some of the things that could distract you from your plan. Maybe a telephone conversation went on longer than necessary. Perhaps you spent too much time in front of the television, and now you need to sprint to fix the meals or clean the house. It helps to have a schedule for your household chores: laundry day, shopping day, cleaning day, and so on. Do not be a slave to your schedule, however. Your schedule is a guide, not the law of the Medes and Persians. Flexibility is always an option.

So what are you going to do with the time for yourself? Perhaps you could spend a few minutes reading a book, exercising, developing a skill, fixing your hair or enjoying a bubble bath. The point is that even if it is only a few fleeting minutes, doing something for yourself should become a habit. This will remind you that you are important and that you deserve to treat yourself well. "But my baby does not take long naps, or if he does, I have to catch up on my chores while I can." This is so true. Well, why not put Baby in the playpen and sit right there and read even a portion of a chapter in an interesting book? Train yourself to find a little bit of time for you. This will prevent burnout.

My favorite word is "delegate." Almost everyone in the family can help with something. Let the tasks be age-appropriate. We are not suggesting that everyone gets to do all the work while you do absolutely nothing! If each person has a task, the burden of taking care of the home gets lighter. Then everyone can be happy. Some two-year-olds enjoy putting clothes in the hamper. You and your four-year-old can set the table and clear it together after the meal. Your younger kids can also help with dusting the furniture.

Study your "body clock." Some of us are morning people, so we can plan to do our heaviest tasks in the morning. If you are a night person, schedule your heavier tasks to suit your evening burst of energy.

Here is another time-saving tip for working moms. You can save time and the stress of finding what you will wear to work if you plan your wardrobe ahead of time. Decide what you will wear to your job for a month (if you do not wear uniforms). Deciding what to wear is often more time-consuming than actually getting dressed. Hang your clothes according to categories. Keep skirts and slacks together. Hang suits together. Hang separates near each other. Hang similar colors together. Then write down different combinations for different days of the week. It will amaze you how stress-free getting ready for work will become. You will find that because of your planning, you will seem to have a more extensive wardrobe.

In her book *Smart Planning,* Sandra Felton shares a useful tip about making use of little slots of time. "Use spare minutes," she advises. "Whenever you have a minute or two, do a little something. Dust, pick up something and put it away, file a paper, replace a light bulb. These are things that can be done in a jiffy. . . . Make this habit a part of your overall program, and the house will stay orderly."

Emilie Barnes also endorses the wisdom of doing things in "small blocks of time." Here is a list of her ideas:

> *What can be done in five minutes:*
> • Make an appointment.
> • Make a party guest list.
> • Fax a note.
> • Write a short letter or note.
> • Water the house plants.
> • Clean out a drawer.
> • Feather-dust the living room.

What can be done in ten minutes:

- Pick out a birthday card.
- Repot a plant.
- Sort out your desk.
- Do a short exercise.
- Call in a catalog order.
- Reorganize the freezer section of the refrigerator.

What can be done in 30 minutes:

- Sort today's mail.
- Skim a report (use a highlighter pen for marking key points).
- Skim your stack of magazines that haven't been read.
- Work on a craft project.
- Make a packing list for a future vacation trip.
- Arrange a school pickup pool, a car pool, or a baby-sitting pool. (*Creative Homemaker* 185).

Do not be intimidated by time. "Time can be your friend if you learn how to make it work as a friend," encourages Emilie Barnes. (184) It is all about planning.

Some Tips about Organizing

Many of us long for better organizing skills. Some people seem to have immaculate houses all the time. I was visiting a friend and was very impressed by her immaculate house. I asked her how she did it in spite of her busy schedule. "Rules" was her answer. "I have rules for everyone." Many of us do have rules for our families, but we sometimes get tired of enforcing them. Either we stick to the rules, or we die from overwork. We do not have to behave like army generals; we can be pleasant and celebrate the benefits of a clean house because everyone in our family cooperated with the rules for keeping the house tidy.

Some people take time out from a tidy house because they have kids. Big mistake! We can teach our kids the habits of tidiness from an early age so that when they grow older, tidiness will not be foreign to them. Imagine a teen-ager having to unlearn bad habits. By patiently teaching and affirming habits of cleanliness and tidiness in our children from an early age, we can avoid constant battles with our teens over keeping their rooms tidy.

Sandra Felton suggests three C's for getting and staying organized; these tips will prove very helpful to us. Here is what she suggests:

Consolidate. Group things together that are alike. "To consolidate means to bring things together or to join things into a whole. . . . Gather each and every one of your belongings into a group of similar things" (38).

Containerize. "Once you see how many items you have of each grouping, you are ready to put the different groupings into containers, such as boxes, baskets, or whatever makes sense from what you have and where you have to place it." (39, 40)

Condense. Get rid of "excess belongings." We are often amazed at how much stuff we have. "It is when we see how much duplication we have, after we have sorted things into groups, that it really hits us. 'I have w-a-a-y too much!.'" (42, 43)

Felton also shares the "smart lazy" idea. Being "smart lazy" is the policy of not expending unnecessary energy. "Stay organized so that I don't have to work so hard. I don't let problems develop. . . . Be smart lazy. Set up your life for success." (35, 36)

Embarking on a plan to be organized involves getting rid of clutter. Clutter stifles. It is a good idea to go on a decluttering campaign regularly. I have found myself hating clutter with such a passion that my husband gets very nervous when he sees me on the rampage. Catalogs, advertisement pamphlets, and junk mail make it to the trash can in record time. There is no point in putting these things down until there is time to study them. Put them into the trash can speedily. It feels good. As we go through our possessions, we find that there is abundance of things—the dress that we hope to wear after we have lost a few pounds, the bags and shoes that do not match anything we have, some broken appliances that hubby planned to fix a decade ago, sheet sets that do not fit any of the beds we now have, and on and on.

Experts advise that we make three groups: things that must be thrown away (and we do that right away), things that are good enough to be given away, and things that we will keep because they are of present use to us. Do not fall into the trap of rechecking the pile of things you planned to throw away, for fear of elevating these items to a position of securing them. If you have not used an appliance or utensil in one year or so, and it has been buried in a remote corner of your house or garage, you need to find another home for it.

Make organizing a science, and you will be rewarded. An organized home is a home with a lower level of stress. You will be able to arrive at some of your own strategies for organizing your life. Then share your ideas. Your friends will thank you.

There are many books and websites that give valuable information on how to be organized and stay organized. Here are some websites listed in *Smart Organizing*, by Sandra Felton: (252)

www.messies.com

http://groups.yahoo.com/group/The-Organizer-lady

www.OnlineOrganizing.com

www.OrganizersWebRing.com

www.nsgd.org

www.napo.net

www.faithfulorganizers.com

One of my favorite books is *Emilie's Creative Home Organizer*, by Emilie Barnes. It has often served as a survival manual for me. Here are a couple of her "Prime Rules of Organization":

1. Use a single notebook for notes and basic written information.
   - Jot down five areas of your life that need straightening; concentrate on these areas.
   - Isolate these basic five areas. You must learn to focus on the part and not the whole.
2. Divide difficult problems into instant tasks.
   - When you see a problem area like a messy refrigerator, don't look at the whole mess, but start with one area of the whole. Clean one shelf or one drawer at a time.
   - If the whole is too large to do in one day, take two or three days to complete the task. You will feel so relieved and proud when you finish. (23)

School Morning Blues

It is easy for our homes to look like battle zones after the kids have left for school in the mornings. If Mom works outside the home as well, then the chaos is multiplied. Mom, here is an idea for you. Encourage the kids to pack their schoolbags and lunch bags the night before. If the children are quite young, you may need to do this for them. Place the schoolbags near the door. This helps reduce the frantic rush around the house for homework papers, pens, pencils, and schoolbooks.

Instead of wearing yourself out by repeating commands and reminding the kids of their routines every day, make an attractive list and put it on the bathroom or closet door. Itemize the things they need to do, in the order in which they should be done. The children just have to look at their lists, and they remain on track. No one will be in danger of forgetting to brush their teeth or hair or leaving the lunch sandwiches behind in the refrigerator. Even kindergarten kids who cannot read can follow the list. I made a list of pictures for my kids when they were in kindergarten. I would put a picture of a shower, followed by the picture of a bowl of cereal, a toothbrush, a hair brush, the bathroom and soap, the lunch bag, the schoolbag, and a pair of lips for the goodbye kiss. Of course I kept an eye on things, but I was not stressed half as much on school mornings. As a working mom, I had to create survival techniques. I survived those years of schooldays with four children.

The Money Manager

At the beginning of our marriage, I had such utter confidence in my husband's financial ability that I paid little attention to money matters. We made a budget and worked hard at sticking to it. We were a two-paycheck family, and that helped us to make ends meet. However, I did not pay much attention to the larger financial picture. During the initial years of our marriage, in spite of Jansen's hints and pleas, I remained happily uninterested in our financial future, resting securely in the thought that I had a husband who could provide for us and who possessed accounting skills.

Then I got wise. I realized that I needed to show an active interest in our spending and in our financial future. What if my spouse became disabled? Suppose I became a young widow? I needed to be financially savvy. I changed my direction and began to show greater interest in our finances. I felt more in tune with life. I had caught a new glimpse of my purpose in life. I had become a real partner in our marriage. This was no longer a one-sided affair.

Some pastors' wives have found themselves in a pitiful crisis because of their husbands' untimely passing. They lacked marketable skills or were inexperienced in managing their finances. Some were even unaware of how much their husbands earned. Others had no idea of the benefits they were entitled to from the organization for which they or their husbands worked. Now that these women were alone, they were helpless.

A woman needs to prepare herself for life. We live in an age where more and more women are preparing themselves professionally to take care of themselves and their families. This preparation is not to be confined to those ladies who choose to work outside of the home. More and more women are deciding to become stay-at-home moms. The important thing is that a wife who is a full-time homemaker must ensure her marketability by improving her skills, taking classes, and doing online and continuing education courses. The idea is to be a prepared woman.

In her book *Taking Charge of Your Life,* Florence Littauer has compiled a list of questions on insurance, tax, and inheritance issues that can be very helpful for women who do not want to wait until it is too late. Here are some of the questions she asks:

- Does your husband have life insurance and do you know where it is?
- Do you know for sure that you are the beneficiary?
- Do you have enough personal life insurance to cover minimal funeral expenses ($5,000)?
- Do you have health insurance for you and your family?
- Do you know what retirement provision you have and who gets what and when?
- Does your husband have an up-to-date will? Do you know where it is kept and who inherits what? Have you seen and read it?

More Money Matters

I like what the Proverbs 31 woman does in money matters: "She sees that her trading is profitable" (Prov. 31:17, NIV). Here are a few money-saving ideas. The first way to save money is to faithfully give God His part of our earnings. Returning our tithes and offerings to God gives us a blessing that we cannot comprehend. Many of us marvel at the elasticity of the remaining portion of our finances after we have been faithful in returning God's part to Him. This is our Father keeping His promise to us. Did He not say, "Bring ye all the tithes into the storehouse . . . and prove me now herewith. . . . If I will not open you the windows of heaven and pour you out a blessing, that there shall not be room enough to receive it" (Mal. 3:10)?

Menu planning is another way to save money; it is especially helpful for working women. This saves not only time but money. It prevents us from running to the grocery store practically every evening after work and just picking up items on impulse, causing additional expense. Also, remember that when you buy your fresh produce in season, you save a lot more than when you buy it frozen or canned.

Try cooking more than one meal at a time. This saves you from standing in front of a stove to create a meal every single day. On weekends and holidays, one can cook some meals in advance for a few days. It is a lot easier to heat up a meal than to cook the entire meal from the beginning.

Coupons are another great financial help. Save and categorize your coupons. Remember to highlight the expiration date. Emilie Barnes shares some insights on maximizing coupons. (*Survival,* 103) Whenever possible, she says, use double discount coupons. Check your newspaper for these coupons. Coupons are wonderful money-savers.

Our children ought to be exposed to managing finances. First of all, teach them to give to the Lord. According to the age of the child, help them calculate the Lord's tithe. A regular allowance for children is another recommended practice. This aids them in money management. Children should be taught to save and to spend wisely. Many experts do not recommend that children get an allowance for doing household chores. But sometimes children do extra chores to surprise their parents. At this time it is appropriate to give them a little token of affirmation. The family is a firm, and in a firm, all partners are supposed to contribute. A loving and caring spirit will motivate children to help in the home. Also, let the older children have an understanding of the expenses in the home. This will make it easier for them to understand the importance of being careful about the use of money and educate them in money management.

Can It Be Done?

So do we have to be stunt women to survive the parsonage? Of course not. We need to plan, study, and prepare ourselves for our tasks. We cannot fill all the gaps and meet everyone's demands. What we must do is ask God for wisdom to function effectively. We can lean on Him and gather strength from Him. "The Lord is my rock, and my fortress, and my deliverer; my God, my strength, in whom will I trust; my buckler, and the horn of my salvation, and my high tower" (Ps. 18:2).

God knows the gifts He has given us. He does not demand that we work feverishly and continuously to the point of burnout. He expects that we share what He has given us for His glory. God also knows the challenges of human relations. He will guide us in these, too. With the love of Christ in our hearts and the guidance of the Holy Spirit, we will be able to have a balanced ministry. God knows the state of our hearts, and He understands our unique situations. Do not despair. There is no need to be a stunt woman.

CHAPTER 5

THE DEVOTIONAL LIFE OF THE PASTOR'S WIFE

You might think that some things are not necessary—like a chapter on the importance of a devotional life of a pastor's wife. That is a myth. Some things *are* worthy of repetition. Often we tend to think that because we are in a full-time employment in the Lord's work, we have a lifetime connection with Him. It is like a "once-and-for-all relationship." Big mistake! Like every other relationship, our relationship with God needs to be nurtured.

Why Is a Devotional Life Necessary?

Many of us experience the need to fill a spiritual void. Perhaps that is why there are so many female worshippers in our churches. We like to pray and sing and lead out in religious events. We hear more about females who are prayer warriors than we do about men organizing prayer groups. Without the filling of the spiritual void, we often suffer from a lack of fulfillment. We find ourselves in search of something. What is it? That something is a relationship with our heavenly Father.

A devotional life also gives us an opportunity for introspection. This yearning prompted the psalmist's request, "Search me, O God, and know my heart: try me and know my thoughts: and see if there be any wicked way in me, and lead me in the way everlasting" (Ps. 139:23, 24).

Imagine some moments in a close encounter with God. We feel comfortable in His presence. We have some undesirable thoughts we dare not share with anyone else. In fact, we urgently want them blotted from our own memories. There in the holy company of the Almighty, we dig deeply into our inmost souls and excise every layer of scum we can recall. We may have had a few unholy escapades of which we are ashamed. We can talk to God about these, too. Then a freedom from fear and guilt envelops us as we "drop off" our filthy rags in exchange for our Lord's cleansing grace. What an experience! Now we can bask in that purging experience because of our Savior's assurance that He will "remember our sins no more." We can enjoy the gift of peace.

Another reason for the importance of a devotional life is that it gives us renewed strength and energy. When we awake in the mornings and are faced with a long to-do list, we are overwhelmed. A feeling of tiredness sweeps over us even before we begin our tasks. That is the time for our private devotions. Meeting with our Lord revives us and gives us courage to face our responsibilities. We arise from our knees feeling restored and invigorated. The Lord imparts His strength to us.

One of the things I like about reunions is that they lead to the renewal of relationships. We may not have been in touch with our friends and relatives for a long time, but meeting them again and sharing our experiences often lead to a commitment to "keep in touch." This is another reason why our devotional life is essential. When we reconnect with the Lord, we get the opportunity to renew our relationship with Him. We may have been neglecting our moments of quiet time with Him; however, after we resume our periods of spending time with our special Friend, we find ourselves enjoying that reconnection. Then we do not want to lose this precious privilege again.

Spending time with God habitually also reaffirms our testimony. Being in God's presence continually has noticeable benefits. It is impossible to walk and talk with God often without tell-tale signs. Enoch walked with God, and everybody knew it. Daniel communed with his heavenly Father every day, three times a day, and the nation of Babylon felt the difference. Spending time with God in private enhances our witness. God's glory and grace are transmitted to us, and we shine before our fellowmen.

Moses' face shone with such a dazzling brilliance after his appointment in the mountain with God that the children of Israel squinted in his presence when he descended the mountain. The connection that Moses had with God showed. "And the children of Israel saw the face of Moses, that the skin of Moses' face shone" (Exod. 34:35). This is amazing! When we spend time with Jesus, people will know it. Our witness will be more potent and effective.

Because we work with people, our influence is important. Satan is ready to dilute this influence. This is why it becomes crucial for us to seek God's presence continually. Ellen White articulates this need very forcefully: "No man, high or low, experienced or inexperienced, can steadily maintain before his fellowmen a pure, forceful life unless his life is hid with Christ in God. The greater the activity among men, the closer should be the communion of the heart with God." (*Testimonies to the Church*, 7:194) Pastors and their wives are in constant interaction with people. Our lives need to be "hid with Christ in God." Our words and actions will demonstrate this, and we will not have to tell people that we have been meeting with God. They will see it. Our faces will be radiant and our demeanor tranquil. We will inspire others. That kind of witness we all desire.

Establishing an Exciting Devotional Life

An important step in establishing a sound devotional life is to realize our need for it. By asking God to reveal this need, we will feel a burden to initiate a devotional habit. Naturally we will want to study and possibly revise our present schedules. By making a list of our daily tasks and the time we allot to them, we get a clear picture of our daily demands. Our lives are crowded with appointments and commitments. How can we fit everything in and still include God in our lives? Here is where prioritizing is mandatory. A good plan is to rank our tasks in descending order of importance; put time with God at the top of the list. We may need to rise earlier in order to meet this new appointment. There are some people, however, who prefer to have their special moments with God at the end of the day. Study your rhythm. Are you a morning person or a night person? Examine your own life and assign a special time for your personal devotions.

Let us review some reminders for establishing a devotional life:

1. Ask God to impress this need upon you. Tell Him you are longing for a closer connection with Him.
2. Study your present schedule and revise it if necessary. We need to plan for our private devotions.
3. Make a personal devotional covenant with God. God can give you the strength to keep this covenant.
4. Evaluate your devotional period from time to time. This prevents us from getting trapped into a dull routine or ritual.

Other factors that will influence your devotional period include the structure of your family. Do you have babies, toddlers, preschoolers, or teenagers? If you have babies and toddlers, you may have to split your devotional periods into installments. A woman who is a homemaker may have a different devotional plan from the wife who works outside of the home. Your devotional program must be custom-made for you. Put your personal plan into effect and maximize the benefits. Ask God for wisdom to direct your new resolution and make a pledge to have regular personal devotions. Then claim God's promise for His keeping power.

The basic tools for our private devotions are the Bible and a devotional book. Sometimes a habit can deteriorate into a dry routine. We want our private time with God to be special and meaningful. We want to enjoy this time with Him. Soft music for meditation is an effective enhancer.

A prayer list is also useful. There are so many people for whom we desire to pray that we sometimes forget a friend here or a relative there. Then, after we arise from our knees, we have to add a postscript to our prayer. A prayer list is a wonderful help. We may divide our list into various columns according to categories of people: spouse, children, relatives, colleagues, people you want to see saved, sick people, the nation's leaders, the leaders of our church, and many other categories. Then we can note the specific needs of these people, e.g., employment, a Christian spouse, success in school, improved health, financial freedom, a home, freedom from fear, restored family relationships, and career guidance; these are only a few examples.

Our daughter Karen-Mae introduced the prayer calendar method to our family. This works extremely well. For example, you may want to pray for unsaved relatives on Mondays, improved health for a spouse on Tuesdays, for a child to return to the Lord on Wednesdays, and so on. A prayer calendar is a helpful item on our devotional tools list.

Different versions of the Bible add variety and even clarity to our Bible reading. Spending time comparing and digesting God's Word is an enriching experience. Text memorization is also very stimulating. Repeating these memory verses throughout the day keeps us in touch with God.

Many of us like journaling. An attractive journal is an incentive to write our thoughts. We can write letters to God. We can express our insights about His Word. We can record our victories and express some of our fears. Journaling helps us express what is in our souls. This is why we want to keep our journals safe and protected from inquisitive or prying eyes. Your journal is your book of praise, thanksgiving, and conversations with God. A journal, therefore, is a wonderful addition to our personal devotional tools.

It is a good idea to keep all items for our devotional period in one place. Highlighters, pens, pencils, and a notebook are also necessary to our personal devotional collection. I recommend a devotional basket. Purchase a simple basket that is large enough to contain all or most of your devotional knick-knacks, and then decorate it with beautiful fabric, ribbons, lace, or whatever your creativity dictates. When you are ready for your devotions, you need only pick up your basket and take it with you. I am blessed to have a beautiful devotional basket that my friend Marta made and presented to me many years ago. Devotional baskets make excellent gifts!

Prayer as a Part of Our Devotional Life

So much could be said about the importance of prayer that this subject cannot be adequately addressed in this little subdivision of this chapter. However, because prayer is the most crucial building block of our devotional life, a major portion of this chapter will be devoted to it. It is the mainstay of our lives. Ellen White says, "Daily prayer is as essential to growth in grace and even to spiritual life itself as is temporal food to physical well-being." (*Messages to Young People*, 115) She also refers to prayer as the breath of life. Just as we cannot live without breathing, we cannot sustain a healthy spiritual life without prayer. It is no wonder that the Apostle Paul urges us to pray without ceasing.

Sometimes we lose balance in our prayer life. There is the temptation to pray only for ourselves. After we have done this, we feel guilty and commit to praying mainly for others. It is very easy to pray for ourselves. We know our needs and our weaknesses. We are close to our desires. So we have a nice long prayer wish list. However, it is equally important to pray for others. This habit of intercessory prayer is necessary. Jesus set the example: "I pray for them: I pray not for the world, but for them which thou hast given me; for they are thine" (John 17:9). Jesus prayed this intercessory prayer for His disciples.

Mothers are especially known as agents of intercessory prayer. There are many stories about the saving effect of a mother's prayer. There is a characteristic persistence and sincerity in a mother's prayer. In *The Adventist Home,* Ellen White endorses with clarity the power of a mother's prayer: "It is impossible to estimate the power of a praying mother's influence. . . . The influence of those prayers is to those children as a wellspring of life." (266) Let us make a commitment to pray for someone every day.

Prayer and Forgiveness

Forgiveness is so connected to prayer that we must spend some time dealing with this important aspect. Not only is forgiveness a gift from God, it is also a prerequisite for going to heaven. Forgiveness is not a naturally easy attribute for us humans. We are familiar with the saying, "To err is human, to forgive, divine." There are two conditions that force one to forgive: offending our fellowmen and offending God. So if we have fallen into one or both of these categories, we need to get on the forgiveness track. As for the reasons for forgiveness, there are three critical ones: the desire to obey God, the example of God, and our eligibility to receive God's forgiveness.

Some important elements embedded in forgiveness are love, mercy, repentance, and willingness. Turning the spotlight on the element of willingness can be very revealing. We refer to a willingness to forget. Forgetting does not imply total memory loss nor an attack of amnesia. Instead, it is a dilution of the intensity of the pain and bitterness that the injury caused. While the offence may still be recalled with a trace of sadness, it is overlaid with a feeling of peace and even victory.

There must also be a willingness to forgive ourselves. It often seems easier to forgive others than to forgive ourselves. How many times have we continually beaten ourselves for something we have done? How often have we hated ourselves? Once we have turned over our guilt and wrong deeds to God and asked His forgiveness, we can accept our Father's forgiveness and enjoy the freedom that comes from forgiving ourselves.

What about a willingness to turn our hurts over to God? I like the invitation, "Casting all your care upon Him; for He careth for you" (1 Peter 5:7). Next, there must be a willingness to pray for the offender and to rebuild a relationship with God. Forgiveness is linked to the spirit of willingness.

There are several benefits to be gained from forgiveness. These include fellowship with Jesus, restoration of relationships, improved personal health, peace that can come only from God, and the opportunity for God to work in our lives. However, above and beyond these benefits is the guarantee of God's forgiveness. In the Lord's Prayer, we read, "Forgive us our debts, as we forgive our debtors" (Matt. 6:12). Jesus clearly explains the crucial importance of forgiveness. "For if ye forgive men their trespasses, your heavenly Father will also forgive you. But if ye forgive not men their trespasses, neither will your heavenly Father forgive your trespasses" (Matt. 6:14, 15).

The conclusion is simple. We will have to stop praying if we do not want to forgive. We pray because we believe that God hears us. God hears us—sometimes. You may ask, "God hears us sometimes? I thought He heard us every time we pray." Well, listen to what my Bible says: "If I regard iniquity in my heart, the Lord will not hear" (Ps. 66:18). Let us follow the sequence of a typical prayer. We express adoration and praise. Then we rehearse His blessings on us. Of course we beg for cleansing or, in other words, forgiveness of our sins. Wait a minute! How can we seek forgiveness from God unless we first forgive our friends, relatives, and neighbors? Then why pray since we have no one to hear us? But, my friend, we want to pray, we need to pray, we need to forgive, and we need to enjoy forgiveness. Forgiveness is not always easy, but always beneficial. Forgiveness is never easy, but Godlike.

Prayer is also a source of strength. Jesus, God's Son, gained His strength from prayer. Early-morning prayer sessions with His Father and 40 days of prayer and fasting were sources of Jesus' strength. It was after Jesus agonized in prayer with His Father in Gethsemane that He gained His strength for Calvary. Prayer gives hope. Prayer gives power.

Prayers of total thanksgiving are also an excellent idea. Try praying a prayer of nothing but thanksgiving. Avoid the temptation to sneak a prayer request or two into this prayer of thanks. Just thank God. It is a refreshing experience.

Praise in Our Devotional Life

Engaging in praise is an exhilarating experience. It is unfortunate that we do not offer profuse praise more often. One of my favorite texts is Psalm 119:164: "Seven times a day will I praise Thee." How about taking this literally? A quota of seven periods of praising God daily is a wonderful habit to form. Try it and feel the difference.

Note that there is a difference between thanking God and praising Him. We thank God for what He has *done* for us. We praise Him for whom He *is*. We praise God because He is our Creator, our Redeemer, and our Protector. We praise God because He is awesome. In *Testimonies for the Church*, Ellen White says, "We must be . . . continuous in our . . . expressions of gratitude to God for His bounties to us" (5:271, 272).

Sometimes we find ourselves limited in our list of things that God is. In her book *My Heart's Cry,* Anne Graham Lotz shares an insightful list of God's attributes. Here are just a few of them:

- He is enduringly strong.
- He is eternally steadfast.
- He is the sinner's Savior.
- He is the breath of life.
- He is the key to knowledge.
- He is the wellspring of wisdom.
- He is the highway to happiness.
- He is indescribable.
- He is the doorway of deliverance. (47, 48)

Constant recognition of who God is fills our hearts with gratitude and peace. A spirit of praise is restorative and therapeutic.

Having a Devotional Life in Spite of the Little Ones

"I would like to have a devotional life, but it is so hard with the kids." Many mothers of young children express this desire. And it is a challenge. Young children are very unpredictable. Just when Mom thinks that Junior is going to sleep until 7:00 a.m., Junior appears on the scene at 6:30 and ready for battle. So Mom decides to take things in stride. She will spend a few moments with God when Junior takes his nap in the afternoon. That is just the day little sister has a tummyache, and by the time Mom gets her comfortable, Junior's naptime has passed. Mom has to start getting dinner ready while trying to put in place 1,000 other things. Whatever became of the devotional time?

Susannah Wesley, the mother of Charles and John Wesley, had 15 children.

Whenever she felt the need for a little time with God, she would put her apron over her head. That was her little quiet "spot" for communion with her Friend. Her children recognized this and kept very quiet.

You might not be able to spend large blocks of time in private devotions if you have young children. Do not be discouraged. Try the bite-sized portions of your spiritual meal as they present themselves. You will still receive the blessing and the refreshing. Be sure not to give up in desperation and stop trying. Jesus will help you. He understands your heart.

Guess what? Those kids will grow up someday, and you will be able to reorganize your devotional life without having to think about the demands of those little darlings. Yes, the kids will grow up indeed; but what about you? Well, you will have grown too—into a spiritual giant!

CHAPTER 6

"TWINKLE, TWINKLE LITTLE STAR"

A family had company over for dinner one evening. When everyone was seated at the table, the hostess asked her five-year-old son, Mike, to ask the blessing on the meal.

"In front of all of these people?" Mike protested. "I don't know what to say!"

"Never mind, dear," coaxed Mom. "Just tell Jesus what you've heard me say."

"Dear God," began Mike, "Why in the world did I invite all these people to dinner!"

Perhaps most of us have felt this way sometimes when the pressures of entertaining descended upon us. When guests are coming, we want to give them our best treatment, and that costs us energy, extra time, and planning—even money. We fear that we will have to transform our abode into a five-star hotel. That, of course, is not necessary and should not be our goal.

Angels at Our Table

There are two extreme approaches to the challenge of taking care of company. We may be courageous enough to face the task head-on, or we may avoid it completely. Most of us take the first approach, perhaps because there are so many instances of hospitality in the Bible. The Bible endorses the practice of hospitality. "Do not forget to entertain strangers, for by doing so some people have entertained angels without knowing it" (Heb. 13:2, NIV). We read the story of Abraham inviting strangers into his house and offering them his hospitality; it turned out that he had entertained angels (Gen. 18; 19; Heb. 13:2). When Jesus and His disciples were tired and desired refreshment and fellowship, they visited the home of Mary and Martha and enjoyed their hospitality.

One day, when Jesus had been preaching to the multitudes, He noted that it was past their lunchtime, so He fed them (John 6:5-12); this time a young lad played the important role of providing his simple meal of five barley loaves and two small fishes. The simplicity of the meal did not deter the lad from sharing. Jesus blessed and enlarged that menu. Children and young people should be encouraged to be hospitable.

Entertainment or Hospitality?

"Entertainment" is described as "hospitable provision for the needs and wants of guests" (*Dictionary.com Unabridged*). In *The American Heritage Dictionary*, "hospitality" is defined as "cordial and generous reception of or disposition toward guests; an instance of cordial and generous treatment of guests."

Since the concepts of these two terms are so closely related, they are often used interchangeably. We notice that they indicate pleasantness, generosity, and kindness in terms of caring for the comfort and well-being of the guests. Some persons consider entertaining to be more impersonal, while hospitality connotes a greater degree of warmth, personal interest, and a desire to connect. The Bible uses both words. For our purposes we will use "entertainment" and "hospitality" interchangeably, recognizing that the most important thing for us as ministerial wives is to accept that we have a privilege of meeting not only people's physical needs, but their social and spiritual needs as well. Hospitality is an opportunity for us to show others that we care and to share the blessings that God has given us. In other words, hospitality is indeed a ministry.

I Would Like To, But...

There are several reasons why many of us are intimidated by the thought of having company come to dine at our house:

I do not know where to begin. Begin by making a decision to be hospitable. Think of the blessings that God has given you and commit to sharing them. Next, make a list of people you might like to have at your house. Remember the elderly, especially those who live alone. Young people also love to be invited to a good, home-cooked meal. College students will gladly grab your invitation. You may also want to include the new mother, someone who is in bereavement, a newcomer to your church or town, or newlyweds. Please do not exclude people with children. You may need to plan some activities for these children if they are quite young. If you have children of your own, they could be helpful.

Above all, present your plans to God. He will direct you and give you the necessary wisdom. It is His plan for us to share our blessings. God takes note of what we do. He is pleased when we give even a "cup of cold water."

My house is not good enough. Whether we live in a mansion or a cottage, we can be hospitable. There is a beautiful story in the Bible about a wealthy woman who not only insisted on entertaining the prophet Elisha, but also, with her husband, built him a guest room and furnished it. Whenever the prophet was in town he was welcome there (2 Kings 4:8-10).

Then there was the poor widow of Zarephath who entertained Elijah out of her meager fare. God blessed her with endless supplies of food. "And the barrel of meal wasteth not, neither did the cruse of oil fail" (1 Kings 17:10-16).

There are a few basic essentials necessary for entertaining: a clean house and tidy surroundings, a few guest towels, a meal, friendly people, and pleasant conversation. Soft music usually enhances the environment. There are also some intangibles that make a home comfortable for guests. Try to make the atmosphere in the home appealing. One does not want the guests to feel overwhelmed by the furnishings. Smiles and a peaceful, unhurried attitude will convey the message "You are welcome here. We are happy to have you." This will add to the comfort of the guests. Praying for the presence of God and His holy angels is a valuable bonus. Some time ago we moved into a new home in a different country. As I unpacked and set up house once more, I asked the Lord to make my home a little haven. *Please surround this house with Your peace, Lord. I would like people who come here to feel their cares roll away.*

God answered my prayer. Several times my friends remarked that they enjoyed peace and comfort in our home. Imagine my delight when a friend commented, "Gloria, your house is like a retreat. I feel so relaxed and refreshed." My heart overflowed with gratitude and praise to God.

When we entertain, we are not staging a display of our acquisitions and skills. Our homes are not showrooms. We want our guests to feel the beauty of God's presence while also feeling revived, refreshed, and relaxed.

My furniture is too old. Old furniture does not disqualify us from being hospitable. A bit of polish or new cushions will make a difference. It is a good idea for us to take care of our furniture from the time we get it. A few simple rules and guidelines will help us preserve our furniture. We can encourage and teach our children to take care of furniture and other possessions, including their own toys. This is not only because things cost money, but also because it is an important value to impart to our offspring. We cannot allow them to carelessly destroy things. Teach them that one ought to take good care of their possessions as well as the possessions of others. Then when we visit other people with our kids, these people will not worry that we are bringing a wrecking crew with us.

I am not sure of all of the rules of entertaining. You are not alone; most of us don't know all the rules either. That is why bookstores abound with literature on this subject. Many magazines, books, and CDs give tips on what is acceptable. Material by experts like Amy Vanderbilt and Emily Post is very popular. Nancy Van Pelt has written an excellent book, *Creative Hospitality*, that is full of helpful hints for successful entertaining. There are many sites online that give information on how to set the table, how to seat guests, how to serve the meal, how to greet and introduce guests, etc.

Do not be intimidated. Gather the information bit by bit, and you will be surprised at how much you can learn. Teach your children some of the rules of entertaining as well. Encourage them to help you set the table. Show them pictures of table settings. The other day I saw a set of placemats with the picture of a place setting. All the kids had to do was place the fork, knife, spoon, plate and glass over the pictures on the placemat, and the setting was perfect. Perhaps you may want to create your own placemats using this idea. This will help your kids to set the table correctly. They will love it.

Another idea is to start a hospitality class in your church. Invite a professional to give a class or two to a group of ladies in your church. Remember to include young ladies in your class. There are people in the hotel industry who make these presentations. It is fun learning some things together; then you will be able to teach others. Besides, your confidence will be developed.

I cannot cook well. Many people who are now excellent cooks started out barely able to boil water. Attend a cooking class. Collect recipes. You can find recipes on cereal boxes and other boxes of food products. Newspapers and magazines also often have recipes. Some television and radio programs share recipes. Always have pen and paper handy for these opportunities. Online recipe sites are also a quick source for recipes. Check *www.allrecipes.com* or *www.cooks.com.* If you go to google.com and type in "recipe sites," hundreds of recipe sites will pop up before your eyes. Recipes vary from breakfast menus to gourmet dinner meals. Then start practicing on your family with simple, easy-to-make dishes and gradually your confidence and skill increase. One word of caution: Do not experiment with a new recipe when you have invited persons to dinner. You could have a disaster if the recipe does not turn out right!

Make a list of the dishes you have successfully prepared, master them, and then choose confidently from this collection when you have to entertain. Sometimes you may want to partner with a friend when you invite guests to dinner or lunch. Choose someone who cooks well and likes to entertain. You will find that your tension will be reduced.

I get very nervous when I have to entertain. One sure way to reduce this nervousness is to plan and prepare well. Start with a list of things you need to do. Then check off items as you complete them. Your list will include cleaning, checking on your towels and tableware, and selecting a tablecloth, placemats, and a simple centerpiece (it does not have to be elaborate; a simple floral arrangement will do). Plan your menu and shop accordingly. Stick your menu on your fridge or on one of your kitchen cabinet doors. That will help you not to forget an item. All you need is a simple, well-balanced meal. When inviting guests, it is also a good idea to find out if they have any allergies or special dietary needs.

You will not want to complicate your life with an array of gourmet dishes; if you desire, you will one day graduate to that level of entertaining. If your children are young, you will need to plan more carefully and prepare for your event well in advance. It is sometimes a challenge to operate between fixing a meal for guests and attending to the little ones if you have no help. Plan, plan, plan. Write little notes to yourself so that you do not forget anything. Then ask God to help you and to bless your efforts. It always works.

I fear people will scrutinize my home. Some ladies think that if one does not have a picture-perfect home, they should not entertain. This is erroneous and places an unnecessary burden on us. Generally, our homes are fine. If we maintain our homes, we should not be stressed by how they look. We vacuum, mop, sweep, dust, clean our bathrooms, and take care of our pets, and we are fine. We also try to reduce our clutter. This makes the house seem a bit more inviting. Remind the kids to put their toys away. We need not worry; most people are so busy enjoying the fellowship that our homes offer that they do not take the time to examine if we have sterling silver or stainless steel, or a Persian rug or fake tiles. It is not necessary to conduct a grand tour of the house either. People who accept our invitations in order to evaluate our domestic situation are not real friends. Guests who focus on the state of our home rather than on the warmth of our hospitality miss the blessing. We must not allow them to deprive *us* of the blessings of hospitality. Cleanliness, friendliness, pleasant conversation, and a nutritious meal are the requirements.

It is a lot of work. Yes, sometimes it is. However, like everything else, there is always a way to beat stress and reduce the amount of work. Have a supply of products on hand for quick meals. Pasta, rice, potatoes, soups, frozen or canned vegetables, and beans are culinary savers. You may compose your own list of things to keep in stock. Be sure to replace them after they have been used. Prepare a few dishes in advance (roasts, patties, casseroles, etc.), wrap them in plastic, and freeze them. I have used holiday weekends to go on a cooking spree. With excitement, I have packed the freezer with multiple dishes. This means that when I have company, expected or unexpected, I am prepared at least in the area of the kitchen. When cooking, be sure to prepare the "extra potato." This means cooking a bit more food so that you can be ready for any unexpected guests.

Instead of having to do a major spring cleaning whenever guests are expected, try maintaining an orderly home as much as possible. Bit by bit, try cleaning parts of your home. It is a lot easier than tackling the whole house at once. Then when you have to entertain, only a bit of touching up here and there will be necessary.

If you have advance notice that you will be entertaining, then you can schedule your preparations and spare yourself some hypertension. Let us therefore cast away our fears of preparing for guests. It really is not that scary.

Some Alternatives

Sometimes our circumstances may not permit us to have people at our homes. We may be temporarily living with a family. Perhaps we may have recently moved and not yet set up house, or it may be an unusually busy period of our lives. Yet we long to engage in hospitality. We can engage in external hospitality. Prepare a meal and take it to someone. Our daughters and their husbands have a wonderful system. Apart from inviting people to their homes for dinner or lunch after church, they prepare meals and take them to people. The wives do the cooking and the husbands identify the persons and transport the meals in disposable containers to shut-ins, the ill, the bereaved—people who for some reason cannot come to their homes.

Potlucks are another easy way of entertaining. When a group of people extend hospitality, the responsibility of preparation is shared, because generally, families bring enough food for themselves and a few more people. In other cases, a planning committee will make assignments to various people or groups. Potlucks can be fun. There is often an abundance of food and a variety of dishes for the guests. Another benefit of the potluck is the opportunity to try new recipes and meet the cooks in person. These potlucks or fellowship dinners can be held at church and "can bring the church family together. . . . A feast offered to those visiting the church can be a means of friendship evangelism. Such meals not only provide a social get-together, but can also serve as an opportune means of nutrition education," advises Nancy Van Pelt. (189)

Another idea is picnic-style entertaining. Prepare a picnic meal and go to a park, relax, and enjoy nature and fellowship. You do not even need to go to a park. You can picnic in your own backyard if the weather is agreeable. This is convenient and fun. Kids like this.

One of my favorite authors said that there is a lot of religion in a loaf of bread. Bake some bread, wrap it with a message of hope, a tract, or a little card, and give it to some street people. You will feel very proud of yourself.

When Company Stays at the House
This involves more planning. If guests are making an emergency stay, we will be happy that we maintained the orderliness of our home. However, whether they stay only overnight or spend a few days, there are some things we might want to have in place:

- Fresh sheets and towels
- Soap or shower gel
- An extra towel or towel set

- Drinking water in the room
- Pen and paper
- A Bible and/or a devotional book
- A flash light in case the electricity goes
- Working locks on the bathroom and bedroom doors

Keep some of these items together in a bag, a basket, a dresser drawer, or in any other place where it is convenient to reach everything at a moment's notice. This will spare you the agony of scurrying around the house. Also there will be no chance of forgetting an item of major importance. Just picture a guest having to remain in the shower to drip dry because their host forgot the towel!

Here are a few optional things I like to have available:
- Some Band-Aids
- A hand mirror
- Slippers
- Lotion
- An extra toothbrush
- A welcome note, sign, or some other token
- A night light in the hallway

Discourage your children from wandering in and out of the guestroom. Explain to them kindly that your guests need privacy and that the guests will also respect your kids' privacy. Let them know that hospitality is a family project. Assure them that you are counting on their help because this is another special event in the life of your family.

If guests share bathroom facilities with your children, you will need to check often during the day to be sure the facilities are tidy, especially if the kids are quite young. In many cases, children of the host share their parents' bathroom. This is a good idea.

Find out when your guests are scheduled to leave. This will help you to plan meals and any other activities. At this point, you can let your guest know the scheduled mealtimes in your home and discuss what may be suitable for them. You want to be as helpful and accommodating as possible.

If there is no guestroom, your guest may be very comfortable sleeping on the couch. The couch of a kind family can offer sound sleep to a weary traveler. It is still important to guard the guest's privacy. Also you will need to remember to keep regular household noises to the minimum so that there will be no disturbance of the guest's sleep.

After It Is All Over

When the entertaining is over, you will have a feeling of satisfaction and want to repeat the venture. The smiles and gratitude of your guests will remain etched in your memory. Feelings of satisfaction and accomplishment will flood your soul. Love in your heart, some common sense, and a commitment to make someone happy were the main ingredients needed to make your entertainment successful.

Your home may not be a five-star hotel, but the warmth and fellowship of your hospitality will be such a powerful witness that your home will twinkle like a little star in your community. Heaven will be pleased. And who knows? You may even have entertained an angel or two!

CHAPTER 7

YOU ARE YOUR HUSBAND'S LOVER

Crowded schedules, multiple engagements and tired bodies make it easy for us as pastors' wives to forget that we are still our husbands' lovers. A friend confided in me that with all the demands of pastoral life, she could not afford the luxury of being a lover. She felt so drained that there was no energy left for her to lavish love on her spouse. I hastened to convince her that it was dangerous to omit that "luxury of being a lover."

"To every thing there is a season and a time. . . . A time to love . . ." (Eccl. 3:1, 8). While we dedicate our lives to serving the parishioners and our community, and while we are committed to maintaining clean, comfortable homes and preparing nutritious meals, as well as taking care of our children, loving our spouses romantically must find a definite slot on our agendas. Many pastoral wives are loyal and supportive of their husbands. We want our husbands to succeed and steadily climb the ladder to excellence. The importance of a wife's contribution to her husband's success is frequently noted. There are also some wives whose poor influence and flimsy support short-circuit their husbands' progress. Then there are those wives who are so busy with professional and domestic assignments that romance eludes them. There is a need for balance—work, play, and romantic moments of the pastoral couple.

Whose Turn Is it?

Clergy couples must take the time to plan for romantic times together. In *Every Minister Needs a Lover*, Eppinger and Eppinger articulate the state of many clergy couples: "We clergy learn how to do our jobs in a professional way—attending committee meetings, composing sermons, conducting church business, visiting the sick, doing denominational work, and being involved in the endless tasks of a minister. Our spouses also have their specific tasks to do, and often we operate very well as a couple in managing our homes, working together in our churches. . . . For any marriage to be genuinely fulfilling, intimacy—the creative, growing experience that unites two people emotionally, mentally, psychologically, spiritually and physically—must be the vital, central core." (16)

Those are very powerful words. Clergy couples must take the time to plan for romantic times together. We are bombarded by the demands of many duties and responsibilities. These we faithfully fulfill. We make lists and schedule appointments. The priorities are attended to. Like the proverbial "squeaky wheel," some items on our lists get our attention. In the midst of all of this, where in our master plan is romance?

One lady confessed her awareness of how romantically starved her husband was. However, she refused to feel guilty because she was also starved! "He never brings me flowers or small gifts of appreciation, so I will not make him feel nice either." So here were two starved people, each waiting for the other to serve first. I could not help but smile as I reflected on the words of our Lord in Luke 7:31, 32: "Whereunto then shall I liken the men of this generation? And to what are they like? They are like unto children sitting in the marketplace and calling one to another, and saying, 'We have piped unto you, and you have not danced; we have mourned to you, and ye have not wept.' " Whose turn is it really?

Try communicating your needs to your spouse. Be honest and open with each other. That should help. We need to admit our need for intimacy, romance, and physical love. Take responsibility for neglecting this important aspect of your lives. This is not a session for blaming, but rather for planning to spend a little bit of time regularly focusing on each other. In other words, start afresh. So, whose turn is it?

Rekindling the Fire

We have all enjoyed the warmth and beauty of a glowing fire, especially during cold weather. We know the importance of fuel to keep that fire burning. The fire of our marriages cannot be maintained without the fuel of love and romance. Mary Somerville reminds us of this: "Women, do we make time for those intimate times together and let our husbands know how important they are to us? If you are frequently too tired, it would be wise to see what other activities could be cut out of your schedule or attempt to rest to prepare yourself for this unifying and pleasurable part of the day of coming together with your husband. Praying for God's strength is also appropriate. He will give you His strength and energy for this sacred aspect of your marriage." (120)

In his book *Keeping the Spark Alive,* Ayala M. Pines emphasizes this concept of working to keep the flame of marital love burning. If fuel is not added to it, sooner or later the flame will burn out. The wise man Solomon states, "Where no wood is, there the fire goeth out" (Prov. 26:20). We need to do all we can to keep our marriages alive and vibrant. When the cold, cruel winds of criticism, hostility, and unrealistic expectations sting us, the warm fires of love, intimacy and sharing of a spouse can warm our hearts and fill us with peace, strength, and comfort.

His Needs

Our men seem so strong and powerful that we sometimes forget that they have needs that they long to have met. Women are not secretive about their own needs. How many times have we not heard a woman complain, "No one around here cares about me! Why can't someone realize that I have needs?" We women are explicit about our feelings and our hurts. It is different with men. Men internalize their wishes and their dreams, and sometimes it is not until we notice a dramatic manifestation that we realize that they are acting out of some kind of need deprivation. Earlier in this book, we mentioned the top five needs of men, according to a needs survey conducted by Willard Harley. They were the following in descending order of importance:

1. Sexual fulfillment
2. Recreational companionship
3. Attractive partner
4. Domestic support
5. Admiration. (183, 184)

Sexual Fulfillment. In one of our seminars for pastoral couples, someone remarked that she was shocked that a pastor would have sexual fulfillment so high on his list of priorities. I was very relieved that she came to that realization before it was too late. A pastor is a man with the same physical and emotional needs of any other normal man. That is why he married a woman. Men unblushingly admit their need for sexual fulfillment. Pastors are no different. Of course they will not throw tantrums in the pulpit and hammer on the lectern while bellowing that they are sexually unfulfilled. However, as wives, we must be discerning enough to recognize this need. Then we must be willing to meet this need.

The solution to marital sexual problems does not lie in a single manual. It lies in a basic loving, caring, unselfish, and reciprocal relationship between husband and wife. Another aid to successful marital adjustment is education. Many times there have been faulty perceptions which have accompanied us throughout our lives. The media, our environment, and even some unpleasant past experiences may have affected our view of sex.

It is helpful to remember that our sexuality was God's idea, "So God created man in his own image, in the image of God created he him; male and female created he them" (Gen. 27). Also, enjoyment of marital intimacy is biblically endorsed. In Hebrews 13:4, we read, "Marriage is honourable, and the bed undefiled." We know that "bed" here does not refer to bedroom furniture but to marital intimacy. A friend of mine told me that when she read this text in the Bible, she was very happy because it freed her from feelings of guilt!

Of course it is the devil's plan to make us feel guilty for enjoying God's wedding gift to married couples. Satan has cheapened sex and circulated extremes in the approach to sexual intimacy. There is either an overemphasis on it, or it is ignored. Christians believe in balance. Happy Christians are well-rounded beings—socially, physically, spiritually, and intellectually. The Apostle Paul very clearly denounces the omission of marital intimacy in our relationships. Husband and wife are to give their bodies in willingness and love to each other. "Let the husband render unto the wife due benevolence: and likewise also the wife unto the husband. The wife hath not power of her own body, but the husband: and likewise also the husband hath not power of his own body, but the wife. Defraud ye not one the other, except it be with consent for a time, that ye may give yourselves to fasting and prayer; and come together again, that Satan tempt you not for your incontinency" (1 Cor. 7:3-5).

Infidelity is often attributed to factors like over-commitment to work, lessened contact with God, reduced time spent with the spouse, as well as Satan's unrelenting campaign to break up marriages. However, neglecting sexual intimacy in the pastoral marriage can lead to infidelity. It is a delusion for pastoral couples to believe that they are immune to the pitfalls of infidelity. In *Heart to Heart with Pastors' Wives,* Colleen Townsend Evans explains that in a society where intimacy is valued but so rarely achieved, "our pastor-husbands who are sensitive, caring, and genuinely interested in parishioners can find their human warmth and godly compassion easily misunderstood." (27) Evans continues, "Many people are needy, and ministers, as well as doctors, therapists, and other 'helper-type' professionals, are vulnerable targets. Pastors are especially susceptible." (28)

We need to help our husbands not fall prey to "strange women." The wise man Solomon gives us wonderful insight which can be applied to our need to seriously regard our role in marital intimacy. "The full soul loatheth an honeycomb; but to the hungry soul every bitter thing is sweet" (Prov. 27:7). We do not want our husbands scrambling for crumbs of intimacy from the tables of other women. Let us make a commitment to each other to keep ourselves "full." We need to protect our marriages with a passion.

Because we live in a world of sin where the attacks of Satan are vicious and constant, there will be instances of relational fatalities. However, we must pray hard and work hard to keep our marriages alive. We must aim at a balanced, systematic approach to preserving our families.

When genuine love, manifested in unselfishness and tenderness, is in the hearts of the couple, each will desire the other. Eppinger and Eppinger share a further insight into sexual intimacy: "To deepen sexual intimacy, a couple needs to enjoy sex in ways that will cause it to feed their love. A marriage is vital to the extent that there is a uniting of these two forms of intimacy—physical and psychological. Satisfaction of the personality hungers of one's mate, particularly his sexual ego needs, is extremely important." (71)

There is much Christian literature on how to enjoy the gift of marital intimacy. It is a good idea to avail ourselves of the benefits of such material. This will not only help us in our personal lives, but we will be able to share correct insights with other couples in our congregations or even in the community.

Anything Else?

There are varying degrees of connections—a wink, a smile, a pat, a squeeze of the hand. I like it when Jansen, my husband, smiles at me. This may seem simple, but it gives me a "warm-fuzzy" feeling. Physical contact, however, is not the only means of keeping the fire burning. Communication is absolutely essential. How often do we share our feelings or our convictions? When was the last time we affirmed our spouses? Do we verbalize our admiration for them? One of the benefits of good communication is that it leads to enhanced friendship with our spouses. It is not enough to *love* our husbands. We must *like* them too. This is what spousal friendship is about. Talking and listening to each other can build bridges. Our communication can embrace a wide spectrum, from serious business discussions to mundane "weather talk" to sharing hopes and fears and dreams.

I recall as vividly as yesterday our first few months of marriage. I am not a very vocal person; I tend to be more introspective. So during the early days of our marriage, I did not express my feelings very much. One day my husband asked me if I had been enjoying our marriage. I thought that that was a strange question coming from him. Had I not shown my delight at being with him? Was I not displaying any honeymoon warmth? What was I doing wrong?

"Well," explained Jansen, "you do not say much. I really do not know how you are feeling."

That really shocked me. For the first time I realized how much I had habitually been immersed in my own thoughts. I needed to share more. I needed to verbalize my feelings. Indeed, I was not married to a prophet. He needed to know what I was thinking, how I was feeling about my new life. From that day onward, I worked on being more expressive and communicative. Now it seems as if my husband has created a monster!

We really need to work on improving our communication with our spouses. It is worth all of our effort and energy. Lovers need to communicate.

Recreational Companionship

Many pastoral couples think of themselves as a team. About a decade ago, a young ministerial couple approached my husband and me, stating that they wanted to discuss something with us. I had no idea of what this "something" was. Well, as soon as we got past some preliminaries, this young couple expressed that they had a deep interest in team ministry. They did not want a fractured ministry. They wanted to work together, to share a uniform interest in souls and be recognized as a pastoral team. It was refreshing to see the sincerity and zeal in their young committed eyes. Team ministry is the goal of many ministerial couples.

In contrast to this couple was a pastoral wife who complained that her husband left her "in the dark" about his ministry. She was clueless about his goals, achievements, and disappointments. She was physically present and by his side frequently; however, she felt left out. "What I long for is to feel like part of the team," she explained. It seemed her husband thought that her participation was either unnecessary or would be ineffective. They needed to communicate on this issue.

All Work and No Play

While many couples work together, they neglect to play together. The family that plays together stays together. Couples that enjoy recreational companionship enjoy a refreshing bond. Try watching your husband's favorite game with him or sharing an interest in his hobby and note how vulnerable he becomes. Put the domestic chores on hold for a while and give him some "playtime." You will be amazed at how appreciative he will be. Our men have a need for us to share recreational companionship with them.

There are advantages to recreational companionship. These times give the couple a chance to reintroduce themselves to each other as ordinary human beings. The professional masks are removed, and you are your natural, relaxed selves. This experience is refreshing and revitalizing.

Engaging in recreational companionship with your spouse reduces the probability of stress and burnout. In *Pastors at Greater Risk,* Archibald Hart interviews H. B. London and defines the difference between stress and burnout: "Stress is primarily a biological phenomenon: too much adrenaline and too much pressure. You're on a high and using too much energy to perform certain functions. You have too many deadlines. And you're often overcommitted. Stress is the loss of fuel and energy that often produces panic, phobia, and anxiety-type disorders." (177, 178) Hart continues by describing burnout: "Burnout is much more of an emotional response. In burnout, the victim becomes demoralized and knows things aren't going right. People aren't affirm-

ing him. He begins to lose the vision he had for his ministry. He loses hope...
Demoralization is a good way to summarize it." (178)

By spending free time with your spouse, by playing together and enjoying each other's company, you can reduce stress levels and perhaps stave off impending burnout. Professional burnout is not the only kind of burnout. There is also burnout in marital relationships as well, which is a real dilemma. Accumulations of stress, disillusionment, and general challenges impact the marriage negatively. This is why recreational companionship is of such importance. Pastoral couples need to enjoy the staying power of recreational companionship. We do not dispute that the "family that prays together, stays together." Add to that, "The couple that *plays* together stays together."

Attractive Partner

Our husbands married us because they were attracted to us. Were they dragged to the altar kicking and screaming? Well, I think not. Men are visual, and before they discovered our internal virtues, there was something magnetic about how we looked on the outside. It is called "packaging." We do not need to be convinced about the effect of packaging. Presentation is important. That is why we take care to prepare and place attractive meals before our family and guests. We choose to shop in certain stores because of how they look, in addition to their competitive prices. Attractiveness has its appeal.

We women like to look and feel attractive. Sometimes we let ourselves go and claim that we are too busy to take care of ourselves. Never should we give up on our appearance. We need to hold on to our commitment to beauty and attractiveness, not merely because of whose wives we are, but more significantly, because of whose daughters we are—daughters of the King of Kings. As royalty and as ambassadors for Christ, we cannot allow ourselves to become careless about our appearance. Some of us need to expend more effort than others, but we must not lose sight of our goal to remain attractive.

Our husbands like us to look smart, and that is reason enough for us to make the effort to be attractive. It may involve taking a good look at ourselves in the mirror. What is the shape of my face? Does my hairstyle enhance or impede? Do I need to take better care of my skin? What about my weight? Is it threatening my health as well as my appearance? I must not forget my teeth.

A beautiful smile can do wonders for one's face. When was the last time I examined my wardrobe critically? Some clothes definitely need to be tossed out because of their historical "value." We are not curators of a museum; we are not in the antique clothing business. Do the colors I wear flatter me? If possible, take a color test. If that is not a possibility, then note the clothes and colors that you wear that bring you rave reviews; these are the best colors for you.

We must not limit our attractiveness to outside the home. Women must make the effort to be attractive *in* the home as well. In *The Adventist Home,* my favorite author, Ellen. G. White, makes a striking indictment against women who are careless about their appearance in the home. "Sisters, when about their work, should not put on clothing which would make them look like images to frighten the crows from the corn. It is more gratifying to their husbands and children to see them in becoming attire than it can be to mere visitors or strangers." (252, 253)

Stacks of dollar bills are not found in every corner of the manse. Therefore, we pastoral families have to budget wisely and spend carefully. How can a woman who has little money or no job find the resources to make herself attractive? First, make a commitment to preserve your attractiveness. Second, devise a plan to earn or save some money to maintain your appearance. Plan and save. Third, refuse to feel guilty about taking care of your appearance. We are not advocating extravagance; we are just reminding ourselves to present our body temples in a pleasing package. Read, talk with consultants, be aware of trends, and enjoy your quest for being beautiful.

Charm also makes us attractive. Physical beauty is not a prerequisite of charm. Charm is an indefinable trait that magnetizes, warms, and revitalizes anyone who comes within its sphere. It radiates from the "charmer" and has a softening influence on the charmed. Charm is not a veneer but an authentic trait of a Christian. Every woman has a measure of charm fashioned to fit her own personality.

There are some mysteries about charm. Can it be caught or is it taught? Charm is personal and cannot be copied, or it will come across as fake. Charm is composed of one's mind, appearance, and feelings, as well as one's own sense of security. Here are some steps towards being charming:

1. Careful grooming.
2. Appreciation of nature (nature softens and refines).
3. Organization of oneself; it is difficult to be charming and confused at the same time.
4. The habit of regularly doing something special for someone.
5. A decision to discard negative thoughts.
6. A sense of humor. This includes the ability to laugh at one's own mistakes.
7. Sensitivity to others' needs.
8. A commitment to treat people as if they are important. Remember they are God's creatures too.
9. A resolution to appreciate and pamper oneself.
10. The refusal to let difficult people make you ugly.

In summary, the Word of God gives us a list of ingredients of charm. "But the fruit of the spirit is love, joy, peace, patience, kindness, goodness, faithfulness, gentleness, and self-control" (Gal. 5:22, NIV).

Beauty or attractiveness is not confined to the external only. It comes from the inside out. A heart in which Jesus reigns will cause an outflow of beauty. People will find us attractive. When I was a little girl we sang the following chorus in our Sabbath School:

Let the beauty of Jesus be seen in me
All His wonderful passion and purity.
O Thou Spirit divine, all my nature incline
Till the beauty of Jesus be seen in me.

Connecting with Jesus and pleading with Him to fill us with His Spirit will beautify our lives, and we will become attractive spouses.

Domestic Support

The fourth need of men as listed by Willard Harley is domestic support. We hardly think that that will be on a man's list. Don't we women complain that we need help with work in the home? For a man, domestic support is more than physical help. I do not imagine that a husband wants his wife to take turns with him in mowing the lawn or attending to the plumbing. Apart from a clean house and meals on time, a man craves a peaceful atmosphere in his home.

Phil was disgusted by the chaos that prevailed in his home. He hated to come home at the end of the day. Oh yes, he loved his family, but the chaotic environment drove him almost out of his mind. He described one memorable evening when he got home to a screaming kettle, a whelping puppy, a two-year-old drummer boy, and a blaring kids' video. He clamped his head with his palms and was just about to beat a hasty retreat out of the door in search of peace and quiet when his smiling wife approached him. "Darling," she calmly commented, "it's been like this most of the day."

I am sure that this mom had endured other variations on the theme of chaos throughout her day. There were probably fighting kids, a whining-two year-old, and the sputtering washing machine that threatened to flood the place. It seems as if mothers are better able to cope with this type of challenge.

We women set the tone for our homes. We all like to enjoy peaceful surroundings. Men do too. They depend on us to offer a pleasant and serene environment. This is one of their needs. It is impossible for one person to create serenity in the home. It has to be a multi-dimensional effort of all the family members. If we cannot enjoy comfort in our own homes, where can we go? "Home Sweet Home" is still a desirable situation.

Admiration

When I was a kid in high school, I read the story of Narcissus, who was one of the most handsome young men in all of Greece. Narcissus knew that he was handsome and wanted everyone to admit and affirm his handsomeness. He was especially thrilled when the young maidens told him that their beauty was surpassed by his good looks. On his way home one day, Narcissus and his friends stopped by a lake to get a drink. There in the lake, he saw the most beautiful reflection he had ever seen. It was actually his own, but he did not know it. Narcissus stayed there for the rest of his life admiring his reflection and saying "Only your beauty may surpass mine." Only his death tore Narcissus away from his reflection.

While men are not nearly as addicted to admiration as the mythological Narcissus, they do enjoy admiration. They do not express this need overtly, but they like to be admired. We wives like to be admired and complimented too. However, when was the last time you told your spouse how wonderful you thought he was? Perhaps he is handsome. Does he dress well? Have you affirmed him about his talents? What about letting him know how secure you and the kids feel when he is at home? You may also state your admiration for his dedication to his tasks and his being a good provider. The last sermon he preached may have been well presented and a blessing to many hearts, including your own. Did you tell him?

It is true that we are so busy keeping up with all of life's demands that there is neither time nor energy left for "frills." Well, your spouse *needs* admiration. This is not a luxury. Make the effort. We must not overlook the possibility of some dear sister who is bursting with admiration for your husband and who may even be bold enough to swamp him with floods of admiration.

When caught in the throes of fatigue and disillusionment, a dose of admiration may ease the pastor's pain. The pastor needs emotional support, and when he is down in the dumps, he is likely to accept it from any source. Pastoral wives dare not risk starving their husbands emotionally.

London and Wiseman, in *Pastors at Greater Risk,* make the following enlightening statement: "Don't miss this important reality: Pastors are especially vulnerable to outside emotional support during seasons of fatigue, frustration, and hopelessness. That's why they must nourish every possible prevention dynamic that flows from a happy marriage." (50) Giving our husbands regular doses of admiration is a "prevention dynamic" that we can and must afford.

What Is A Real Lover?

So do we have to take a checklist of our husbands' needs everywhere we go and feverishly rush around attempting to fulfill all of them? This certainly seems like an impossible assignment. The idea is to be cognizant of what a man feels and needs. An awareness of these factors can serve as a road map to direct us to our spouses' expectations and vulnerabilities.

Multiple needs exist in a marriage. Husbands—and wives—have characteristic needs. We wives must not be afraid to identify our needs and communicate them to our husbands. When we are committed to understanding each other's needs, we are on the road to happiness in marriage. No one can fulfill all of our needs all of the time. No one possesses the energy, will, or desire to do this on a round-the-clock basis. Only Jesus can fulfill all of our needs. Let us lean on the assurance, "And my God will meet all your needs according to his glorious riches in Christ Jesus" (Phil. 4:19, NIV).

What does love in a marriage mean? Love in a marriage does not mean that there is an absence of conflict or disagreement. Spouses are independent thinkers from differing backgrounds. That the couple commits to working hard to develop the skills to deal with conflict or disagreements is important. As the years progress, the couple matures, and this maturity brings with it accompanying changes in them. This does not mean that the love is diluted. "Love is not a fixed state of mind," say Eppinger and Eppinger, "but an active and fluctuating interaction between two people whose feelings are continually evolving, creating new configurations and patterns reflecting both continuity and change." (76)

A marriage can only succeed on real love. In *Real Love in Marriage,* Greg Baer declares, "Real love isn't *one* of the most important elements in a happy marriage; it's *the* most important—by far." (189) Being a real lover involves a willingness to work hard on the relationship. This results in multiple rewards. Today is a good time to commit to being your husband's lover.

CHAPTER 8

RELATIONSHIPS, RELATIONSHIPS

Many a minister's wife has battled with questions about relationships. *How friendly should I be with parishioners? Is it appropriate to have close friends? What are the suggested criteria for choosing friends? What if these "friends" turn out to be unfaithful to me? How will my relationships impact my husband's ministry?*

Is there anyone who can exist happily without friends? We all need someone with whom to share. There are those who claim that they do not need others. I think that these people are lonely and do not even know it. One does not need a gang of fans following them perpetually to be happy. We have all heard of the possibility of loneliness in a crowd. Crowds do not provide happiness for us. Sterling relationships can be very valuable, though. Dorothy Kelley Patterson aptly expresses some of our fears about, as well as the importance of, friendships:

"Close ties to others are essential for everyone, but it is hard to know with whom you can trust your feelings and frustrations. . . . Everyone is vying for social engagements, fellowship, and conversation with the pastor and his wife. Isolation seems impossible in such a setting; yet it is inevitable when you do not build intimate friendships within the setting where you spend most of your time." (187)

It is undesirable for us to force ourselves into believing that we ought not to have friends. The pastor's wife is usually living far away from her family and friends. Naturally, she misses those connections and can, at times, become very lonely. Birthdays, anniversaries, and holidays are often spent in surroundings where there is no family. At these times, a yearning arises in our hearts to reconnect with our loved ones. Becoming a pastor's wife, however, does not demand that we sever old connections and resist new ones.

God made us social beings. He wanted us to enjoy relationships; that is why He made a world full of people. Jesus had friends. In fact, He had some close friends, too. In John 11, we read about the fatal illness of Jesus' friend Lazarus. Mary and Martha, sisters of Lazarus and friends of Jesus, sent this urgent message to Jesus, "Lord, behold he whom thou lovest is sick" (John 11:3). The Greek word for "love," translated here, is not *agape* but *phileo*.

In many instances in the New Testament, John the disciple of Jesus is referred to as "the disciple that Jesus loved" (John 19:26; 20:2; 21:7, 20). The translation of "love" here is also not *agape* but *phileo*. This is the love that implies friendship. Jesus did not confine Himself to the multitudes; yet at no time did He lose His focus on His mission. Our Lord knew the benefits of withdrawing from the crowd and taking time out from serving. He spent time with a few intimate friends, thereby refreshing Himself to reenter the rush of service.

Pastoral couples are constantly giving and ministering. We tend to put the interests and needs of our church members in front of our own wishes. We do not complain because we believe that we are called to serve. However, our call to service is not intended to make us social invalids or religious hermits. The Lord of our lives wants us to enjoy life and to be happy, fulfilled servants. He wants us to laugh, to celebrate, and to glory in our assignments. He wants us to rejoice in our ministry. Each of us needs a special friend or two. Each woman is unique and may be able to offer her own special brand of friendship to the minister's wife. The challenge lies in our choice of friends. Our aim should be not to form cliques. Cliques erect barriers and foster prejudices. Christian relationships breed comfort, affirmation, and growth. It is therefore important to give attention to the area of relationships.

True friendships must be tended and nurtured. Extremes in relationships can be damaging. A healthy friendship does not grow in the atmosphere of aloofness and indifference. Nor can a suffocating relationship blossom into happiness and enjoyment. There must be balance. The wise man Solomon presents the two ends of the spectrum of a relationship. "Seldom set foot in your neighbor's house—too much of you, and he will hate you" (Prov. 16:25, NIV). On one hand we see that unbearable frequency can result in a tiresome relationship. On the other hand, the wise man declares, "A man that hath friends must show himself friendly" (Prov. 18:24). Maintaining friendships takes energy, consistency, and effort. An important ingredient in every successful relationship is balance.

Why Relationships?

We are related. We pray "Our Father, which art in Heaven." This means that we are related. We are sisters. This connection is of God. This means we are family. It was God who established the concept of relationship. It is therefore our responsibility to study the importance of these human ties and hone our skills to preserve positive relationships. There are definite advantages to relationships. We gain emotional and spiritual support from our friends. "Two are better than one; because they have a good reward for their labor. For if they fall, the one will lift up his fellow: but woe to him that is alone when he falleth; for he hath not another to help him up" (Eccl. 4:9, 10).

We women are relationship-oriented. We like to share. We talk about our children, our spouses, our parents, our childhoods. We discuss fashion, our homes, and our dreams. We naturally like to share our feelings. We know that we need to guard what we say, and as pastors' wives, there are numerous benign things we can talk about. However, our motto must be beauty of speech. We often cry together and like to laugh together. Women often pray together. We need relationships. Women were meant to interact socially. God made us that way.

Having friends contributes to our healthy existence. We know that people who live in solitude die faster than those who do not. That is why it is recommended that elderly folk who have no companions need to at least have a pet. Sound relationships are good for our health. Relationships also lead to social growth. We learn from each other. By associating with others, we can improve our social skills, learn successful domestic coping secrets, and be inspired to explore new vistas. Through our associations we can mentor someone. Mentoring is recognized as a valuable practice nowadays. Mentoring, however, is not a new concept. In Titus 2:4, 5, we are urged to "teach the young women to be sober, to love their husbands, to love their children, to be discreet, chaste keepers at home, good, obedient to their own husbands." Women in the manse have a wonderful opportunity to mentor. However, we cannot mentor across a gulf. We have got to get close. We must have a relationship.

Things That Damage Relationships

There is hardly anyone who has not experienced or seen the pain that comes from broken relationships. Sometimes relationships that begin pleasantly and are well-meaning land on the rocks. The result is a painful heart and the determination never to get "caught" in any relationship again. Brokenness and deception in relationships leave people devastated and disillusioned.

Dishonesty damages relationships. Beautiful relationships blossom in an atmosphere of honesty and integrity. We need to choose friends who are not shady in their behavior or mindset. Purity and honesty enhance one's personality. Integrity is also a respectable virtue. Integrity is admirable and Christlike. Dishonesty damages relationships. That is one disqualification from a relationship.

Gossip destroys. We really want to keep far from those who gossip. Being close to a gossiper is like walking on thin ice. There is always the possibility of slipping through a crack into the icy waters of the death of a relationship. Gossipers entrap and ensnare. Tongues can be dangerous. One is not easily cured from the habit of gossip. Victims of gossip are not easily restored either. Gossip damages relationships.

Lack of confidentiality is not conducive to successful relationships. It is not easy to keep a secret. Often the tongue itches to share information that should be kept confidential. Not everyone finds it easy to keep confidences. We need to prove the level of confidentiality of a person before we attempt to share some things. In fact, in some cases, it is better to keep some things to ourselves. Our private thoughts, opinions, evaluations of people, our weaknesses, and our spouses' weaknesses belong within our own hearts. It is a good policy to share only those things that we would not blush to own if revealed to public ears. Share only those things that would not evoke a stuttering and stammering defense from us. Confidentiality is a solid pillar of a successful relationship. Not many possess this gift.

Competitiveness undermines relationships. It has its roots in sin. It was the competitive spirit of Lucifer that urged him to start a rebellion in heaven. One cannot see the virtues of another through competitive eyes. The competitive spirit is a restless spirit. The competitive person thrives on bitterness, comparison, and even devious behaviors. There is hardly any beauty in the heart of the person who surrenders their mind to the competitive spirit. The bitterness of competitiveness threatens not only the object of one's competition but also destroys the one who dwells in that mode. A person who has a competitive spirit is not only unhappy, she is also unwise. Let us see what the Apostle Paul says: "But they measuring themselves by themselves, and comparing themselves among themselves, are not wise" (2 Cor. 10:12).

There will always be someone else who is smarter, more beautiful, and more efficient. Our duty is to affirm and celebrate the talents and virtues of others. The competitive spirit leads to envy, then to hate. Envy manifests itself in thoughts like *I wish I had what she has*, and *I wish she was not that lucky to have it*. In the case of Cain in the Bible, envy led to the murder of his brother, Abel. It is far better to rejoice in the success of others than to torture ourselves with envy.

God has given us all talents. We need to search for those talents and refine and improve them so that we may bless others. As long as we remember that our aim should be not to do better than the other person but to be the best *we* can be, we will experience happiness. This is what Jesus expects of us. He can help us perform with excellence. So there is no need to nurture a competitive spirit.

Recognizing Good Relationships

So far we have established that we humans need to enjoy relationships. It is not God's plan for us to be isolated and solitary. God wants us to enjoy social health. He wants us to be happy Christians. With happy countenances and swift, light steps, we can be powerful witnesses for Him. We do not want to be hindered by heavy hearts from broken relationships. We want to be models of a group of people who love one another.

What are some of the things that characterize a sound relationship? *Thoughtfulness and sensitivity* are valuable components of a good relationship. We want to feel the pain of our sisters, and we think about what they are experiencing. By thoughtfulness and sensitivity we think for and feel for one another.

Loyalty is another sign of a good relationship. A beautiful biblical model of loyalty is exhibited in the friendship of David and Jonathan. Jonathan did not allow the hatred of his father, King Saul, to dilute his friendship with David. A loyal friend is one who does not forsake us in times of adversity. A loyal friend does not avoid us when we become unpopular. Loyalty stands the test of all phases of our life. Loyalty prevails when we are in the limelight of success or in the throes of disaster. "A friend loveth at all times, and a brother is born for adversity" (Prov. 17:17).

A relationship has a price. Not only does a relationship merit the intangibles, like love and loyalty, but it also thrives on tangibles. What do we give in a relationship? One way to preserve a relationship is to *be generous*. Sometimes a card or letter of affirmation can enhance a relationship. In other words, we should not forget to give. Think of something to give to your relationship. People like receiving. We must remember that people who get things are happy, but those who give are happier. "It is more blessed to give than to receive" (Acts 20:35). Let us look for opportunities to give. Sometimes we have to practice giving. Giving can become a habit. Giving is wonderful. A gift does not have to be expensive or exquisite; it only needs to come from the heart. Giving blesses the giver. Try it.

People like to be affirmed. *Affirmation* is a not only necessary for us to enjoy life, it also enhances a healthy relationship. We all enjoy affirmation. Say a few words of affirmation to your children and see how their faces light up. Try affirming the ladies or other workers in your congregation and notice how much harder they work. Affirm your friends and observe the energies they will exert to support you. When was the last time you affirmed your spouse? The pastor needs affirmation from his family. He is exposed to so much criticism that a few generous doses of affirmation will soothe his troubled soul. Affirming somebody every day is a good way to strengthen relationships. We can also affirm by celebrating the successes and victories of our family and friends. Celebrations add color and strength to our relationships. Therefore, it is important to celebrate in our relationships.

Confidentiality exists in a good relationship. We must be able to keep confidences, and those we choose to be our friends should pass the test of confidentiality as well. How can we tell if we are being confidential? Here is a simple test:

1. Don't say it if it will damage or ruin a person.

2. Don't say it if you promised not to repeat it. (Note: If a person confides in you that they will hurt someone, including themselves, let the person know that you cannot promise to keep that a secret. You need to take the necessary steps).

3. Ask yourself, "If I repeat this, will it help someone or will it hurt someone?"

Observing confidentiality is very difficult. However, God has promised us wisdom and strength to achieve our goals. He will also answer our prayer, "Set a watch, O Lord, before my mouth; keep the door of my lips" (Ps. 141:3).

A *forgiving spirit* is another essential ingredient in a good relationship. In close relationships, it is easy to hurt and be hurt. Some hurts go deep into the core of our heart. How can we forgive when there are emotional scars that remind us of what someone has done to us? A relationship cannot survive if there is an unwillingness to forgive. Forgiveness does not mean that we develop amnesia and completely forget the wrong that was done to us. When we decide to forgive, we give up our right to retaliation and vengeance. We no longer dwell on the injustices with acute feelings of anger and pain. We claim the assurance that Jesus, who said, "Vengeance is mine," will take care of the situation (Rom. 12:19). So we turn our hurts over to Him.

Depending on the depth of the hurt, feelings of forgiveness may not be instantaneous. Time, however, helps with healing. As we go to God, He will provide the healing that we need. We do not have to feel guilty because the pain does not disappear overnight. However, when we are hurt by someone, we must eventually rise above it, like Joseph in the Bible who was sold into slavery by his own brothers. The Holy Spirit will help us to genuinely forgive.

We can ask God to give us His sustaining grace to see us through the hurt (2 Cor. 12:7-10). God is able to give us strength for any situation. It is important to feel the urgency of forgiveness because an unforgiving spirit can make us bitter and ugly. Often we are the ones with disfigured hearts, and the offender does not seem affected. Yet we must not allow ourselves to become showpieces of bitterness. The Apostle Paul warns, "Let all bitterness and wrath and anger . . . be put away from you" (Eph. 4:31). Jesus' command to "pray for those who mistreat you" (Luke 6:28) is also very helpful in not only effecting change in our enemies, but also in filling our hearts with peace. It helps us to look away from the pain inflicted on us to the greater work that God is trying to do for us.

It is not necessary for us to withhold our forgiveness until the one who has offended us seeks our forgiveness. Stephen, the first Christian martyr, prayed for forgiveness of his executors while he was being stoned (Acts 7:54-59). There is an invigorating freedom that we enjoy when we extend forgiveness. The peace of God floods the chambers of the soul, and the spirit soars on joyful wings. We need to forgive because we ourselves cannot exist without God's forgiveness. God will not forgive us of our sins if we do not forgive one another. This makes our forgiving spirit crucial to our salvation.

We have a forgiving and merciful God; that is why we can rejoice in the assurance of sins forgiven through the blood of Jesus. It is not always easy to forgive, but it is always right. Let us invite the spirit of forgiveness into our relationships and enjoy the blessings that follow.

Grace and Relationships

There are several factors that combine to produce healthy, happy relationships, but grace outshines them all. This is because grace is a gift from God. God's grace has the miraculous power to sweeten our relationships. We often sing about the "amazing grace" of God. This grace can be present in our relationships only if Jesus is the center. In his powerful book *Captured by Grace*, David Jeremiah says that "grace is a five-letter word that is often spelled J-E-S-U-S." (21) This powerful element comes from God, who saves us by His grace through Jesus. Grace will flavor our conversations. Grace will generally control our actions.

Our relationships may have been shaky or tempestuous. Our faith in humans may have been shattered. Memories of past broken relationships may still be haunting us and restraining us from enjoying new relationships. There is healing power in grace. Grace is restorative. No matter what the past may have been like, or as David Jeremiah comments, "No matter what we have done, no matter the depth of our transgression, the darkness of our hearts—grace overrules them all." (21)

CHAPTER 9

YOU CAN DO IT!

The other day I asked some pastors' wives to share two reasons they had for marrying a minister and their perceptions of the ministry before they got married. I requested that they give me one serious reason and one not-so-serious. It was interesting to observe that many of these pastors' wives were not even willing to *try* to think of a flimsy reason or perception. I was trying to encourage them not to take life too seriously, but I almost felt as if I had made a sacrilegious request.

I ventured my two reasons: I felt I could contribute to the ministry not only because of my talents but also because I had always had a passion for service in the church. They waited on the edge of their chairs for my frivolous reason. I had two. I told them I had an attraction to large, fancy hats. My clerical position would permit me to flaunt such showy head-coverings. Also, with the multiple moves that pastoral families made, I stood a wonderful chance of seeing the world.

When I asked them about some things in ministry that peeved them, several items were shared with rapidity, including the topic of being invisible.

You Can Do It Even If You Are Invisible

When was the last time you felt invisible? This is not difficult for a pastor's wife. What does it mean to become invisible? Many of us do not plan to be invisible. It just happens. Having experienced invisibility myself, I quite understand this state. I rejoice that it is not permanent. This is how it happens. The pastor and his wife are standing together. People greet him and ignore her. Why? Because she is invisible.

This was something I had difficulty accepting when I was a young pastor's wife. Oh, there were visible things that I did, like singing, playing the piano, and directing the choir. I even gave little presentations. I openly supported my husband and the program of the church generally. Why should this invisibility be thrust upon me?

There were times, I must confess, when I really wished to be invisible but had no such luck. In order for one to become invisible, certain prerequisites must be met: A woman must be a pastor's wife, she must be in the company of her husband, she must attend functions *without* her husband. Those are the most favorable conditions for invisibility. A widowed or retired pastor's wife can also qualify for invisibility. The telephone calls lessen, and the attention wanes.

By now you have noticed that I treat this invisibility issue humorously. This was my survival technique. There are different ways of handling being slighted by church members. I have tried most of them. One could get very upset and nurse hurt, angry feelings. Another temptation is to avoid the saints. It even feels good to consider not attending certain events where invisibility may take place. Complaining to some husbands does not help. A number of wives have told me this. How could a permanently visible agent understand the plight of an unseen being?

It took a few years before I learned to cope with my invisibility. I could not understand it. People would look straight through me as if I did not exist. Well, I was invisible, remember? One day I attended church alone. A dear little man met me in the foyer. Without a word of greeting he asked, "How is Pastor Trotman?"

I decided to use my invisible voice to speak up this time. "Oh, never mind that. I am here." I was making a bold attempt to banish my invisibility.

"Is Pastor Trotman OK?" persisted the brother.

I was determined not to remain invisible this time. I was going to fight for substance! I was tired of this ethereal existence. "Well," I replied, feeling confident that my change of state was imminent, "how come you do not ask about me?"

A strange blankness crossed his face as if he had seen a ghost. *At least I am beginning to emerge into substance,* I thought. "Well, please tell him I asked for him" was the parting comment as the little man beat a hasty retreat.

I felt defeated and deflated. "Yes, of course," was my faint reply as I turned on my invisible heels and screamed inaudibly in my heart, "Look at me. I am here. Can't you see me?"

I pondered this "pain" in my breast for a long time, especially since there were many other occasions when I felt unnoticed. I never even made the observation to my husband. How silly of me!

One day, I became wise to the fact that while I was the invisible one, Jansen, my husband, was not omniscient. I was not invisible to him. He had no way of knowing about my discomfort unless I shared it with him. I was always in his eyes and heart. Eventually I did share my plight. What a difference it made! It was as if someone had broken the magician's wand, and no one was able to make me invisible from thenceforth. My husband made certain that I was always properly introduced and made welcome. At the slightest hint of my not being noticed by anyone who came to speak with him/us, Jansen promptly presented me. Once more I had become flesh and blood in the eyes of the church members. It was a good feeling, and verbalizing my discomfort to my husband certainly made a difference.

The next time someone raises a wand to make you invisible, do not let it bother you. It is not your fault; it is theirs. Let your husband know how it hurts. Observe to him that, as part of the team, you deserve to be treated with courtesy and respect. Encourage him to make a point of presenting you and not allowing you to be slighted. Then continue to be your sweet self. You will not be invisible for long, and your ministry will continue to be effective.

Some People Will Love you

There are some people who love the pastoral family. God has placed some people in our paths to minister to us. That helps to make our journey smoother. Many of us, I believe, can remember persons who were always there for us in our ministry. I recall very vividly people who have made our journey less arduous because of their love, caring, and prayers.

It is easy to dwell upon the hardships of the ministry. There are so many people who criticize us and make life difficult for us. However, we must not let negative things mar our happiness. While there may be some who seem bent on making our lives miserable, there are also angels of mercy. We must look for these people and affirm and thank them. We also need to pray for them. Some people love us because of things we may have done for them. Others love us from the beginning, even before they really get to know us. They love us because we are the ministerial family.

Others have grown to love us. They have worked and played with us. We may have been their support in times of crisis. We may have helped them with weddings, family reunions, and baptisms. Our husbands may have even performed the funerals of their beloved relatives. They love us.

There are things we can do to show that we value the love of these people. Do something special for them. Remember their birthdays, their anniversaries, and special events in their children's lives. Call them on the phone and let them know that you appreciate their love; tell them that you are praying for them. Finally, thank God for parishioners who love you.

Some People Will Not Arise Up and Call You Blessed

In spite of how virtuous we may be, the critics will have a campaign about us. There are two major reasons for this:

- Everybody will not like us.
- We have our flaws.

Even if we were perfect, there would still be people who would despise us. Jesus was despised, so we are in good company. People may detest us for different reasons or for no apparent reason at all. I know of a young lady who hated her classmate because he resembled her abusive father. Another girl wished her roommate would die because she was beautiful. One young lady confessed that she hated her cousin because she was still a virgin. People hate for many different causes. Some people enjoy making others miserable and uncomfortable. All of these manifestations are the result of sin and the interventions of Satan, the author of discord.

In ministry as in other areas, there will be multiple criticisms hurled at the pastor and his wife. It does not help to wither under the heat of criticism. We know that criticism is never welcome and hardly ever couched in pleasantness. There are, however, a few things we can do in the face of criticism. One way of dealing with criticism is to ask ourselves the following questions:

- Is there any truth in this criticism?
- How am I contributing to this?
- What can I do to quell this criticism?

If there is absolutely no truth in the criticism and it is unfounded and malicious, we still need to be careful not to give even a semblance of justification for it. Do not let it torture you. Jesus vindicates us. Sometimes, criticism—even unfounded—can be an early warning to save us from impending danger.

If there is an element of truth in the criticism and we are contributing to it, then we need to evaluate our actions very carefully. It may help to have an objective person point out our flaws so that we can start working on that behavior. One effective way to quell this criticism is to demonstrate a change in behavior. We must not let criticism make us bitter and ugly. That will dilute our Christian influence.

We need to remember that even when we change our behaviors, people's memories are long. Jesus forgives and does not remember our past, but humans do not forget although they may claim to have forgiven. We just have to claim God's cleansing power and His promise to "restore . . . the years that the locusts hath eaten" (Joel 2:25).

Moments with God

We cannot be successful without the strength that comes from God. Sometimes our busy lives crowd out the precious moments that we could spend with our heavenly Father. This is sad. A pastor's wife needs to walk and talk with God daily. This is her best method for survival. Only moments with God can sustain us when things seem dark and frightening, our hearts are heavy, and our minds are clouded with disappointment, pain, and frustration. There is a peace that we enjoy after spending time with God.

God made us women with a need to connect with Him. Perhaps that is why so many prayer movements are spearheaded by women. We often hear about praying moms, and prayer breakfasts and prayer vigils organized by women. Many of us have prayer partners, and we keep prayer journals. God made us this way. He longs to meet with us in our quiet moments. In these moments, we can search our souls and seek cleansing. Meditating on Psalm 51 is a cleansing exercise that can be very helpful.

It is easy to attempt to transact our business in our own strength. Appointments at church and in the community crowd our schedules and demand much of our time. Sometimes we forget that we need time for cleansing. Clogged minds and hearts hinder the outpouring of the Holy Spirit in our lives. We cannot afford this. We must stop and ask God to tell us who we really are. We need to ask for forgiveness of our sins. We need to forgive others too.

Ministry can be draining. Challenges and commitments can weaken us. So many people depend upon us for help and support. We ourselves need strength. We need to go to a filling station. I observe that taxi drivers spend a longer time than many other drivers at the gas station. Many of them fill their tanks. Other drivers tend to put just enough gas to keep them going. Imagine a cab driver who takes passenger after passenger to their destinations. He is so committed to his job that he does not spare the time to fill up on gas. One day his cab is bound to stall because he is out of gas. It is also likely to stall at a busy intersection.

We cannot be constantly giving without replenishing. We must fill up if we are to serve. In the presence of God, there is strength for renewal. Let us not deprive ourselves of this blessing.

I like the opportunity that private devotions give us for cementing our relationship with God. The more we meet with Him, the closer we get to God. We are able to develop intimacy with God only by frequently meeting with Him. There is a sweetness that we enjoy from communing with Him. Jesus becomes a Friend to us. We are able to tell Him big things and little things. He becomes near, real, and dear to us. I like that. Connection with God is the ultimate relationship.

Spending time with God never goes unrewarded. Our objective should be to do everything we can to enjoy these wonderful and blessed moments with God. Our strength is renewed. Our mission is clarified. Our purpose is redefined. We now feel ready to face any challenge. So there is no need to feel socially unfulfilled in our ministry. God is on our side, and He will direct our steps.

CHAPTER 10

STRESS, STRESS, EVERYWHERE

"You are no fun anymore, Junie," accused her husband.

These words stung as the hard-working wife tried to analyze the statement. *My husband finds me boring. I try to keep things going well in our home. I cook, clean, take care of the children, and keep our appointments. I also work outside of the home at a very demanding job—only to make ends meet. Now I am "no fun anymore." This is not the award I was hoping to receive.*

Junie, a professional woman, was in her late forties and worked at a large firm. Her husband had climbed the ladder of success in his pastoral career, and together they maintained a successful middle-class lifestyle. Their children were typically lively teenagers who attended a private school and somehow managed to keep themselves out of trouble. The home seemed to be happy from all appearances. However, Mother was "no fun anymore."

In addition to her regular home-making responsibilities, Junie's schedule was packed. The children had commitments of their own which involved the services of Junie's SuperMom Taxi Service. There were piano and band lessons, swimming lessons, and gymnastics. All of these activities devoured five afternoons every week. Even holiday weekends were full. Often the children had to attend weekend camps or engage in volunteer projects. Life was one cruel carousel, and Junie was "no fun anymore." What was the reason for this?

Junie realized that she was often suffering from fatigue. She battled with frequent headaches and caught the flu whenever it came to town. A closer look at herself revealed that her cheerful spirit was waning, and her stomach was sometimes tied in knots for no apparent reason. She dragged herself out of bed every morning and willed her way to work. At night she tumbled into bed, a worn-out mass. Day after day, life seemed devoid of meaning. Her forty-eighth birthday was approaching, and so was menopause. She feared that her life was spinning out of control. Junie was often weepy and irritable. These feelings alarmed her to such an extent that she visited her doctor.

Then came a shocking revelation! She was dangerously hypertensive, over-weight, and teetering on the edge of a physical breakdown. Her physician pointed out that her program was too demanding and that she needed to slow down. "Take some things off your plate," advised the doctor. "Learn to limit your commitments and take up a hobby. Stress is killing you!"

The story ended happily. Junie is a different person today.

This Thing Called Stress

Stress is commonly defined as wear and tear on one's body. In *The Complete Idiot's Guide to Managing Stress,* Davidson defines stress as "the psychological and physiological reaction that takes place when you perceive an imbalance in the level of demand placed on you, and your capacity to meet that demand." (18) Constant pressure from life's demands weighs heavily upon us, and we become worn and feel like a wafer. We may be facing a challenge, and we wrestle with our ability to face it and win.

If there is one person who is prone to stress or pressure, it is the minister's wife. *People* (Friday, March 31, 2006*)* quotes married clergyman and Tennessee marriage therapist Kenyn Cureton as giving the reason for the pressures on a preacher's wife. She is expected to be a "gracious host, a good cook, a good home manager, and the mother of well-behaved kids." Cureton continues, "People scrutinize you because you're the first lady of the church. Everyone in the family is under a microscope." Cureton was commenting on the recent ministry murder in the United States that shocked the nation. Cureton, who has counseled many pastoral couples, has noted that stress in the parsonage tends to lead to divorce, separation, chemical dependency, and even suicide.

Auerbach and Grambling define stress as "a set of changes that people undergo in situations that they appraise as threatening to their well-being. These changes involve physiological arousal, subjective feelings of discomfort, and overt behaviors." (3)

Occasions, events, or circumstances that cause stress are called "stressors." Stressors may be *acute* (events that are brief) or *chronic*. Chronic stressors continue for extended periods of time without any clear definition of their beginning or end.

Stress is not always bad. There is good stress (*eustress*), and bad stress, often referred to as *distress*. Good stress is what keeps us going after a particular goal or project. Perhaps we may be planning a wedding, a church building program, or a big clean-up drive. We may have a series of seminars to present or an exam to take, so we work hard at achieving success. Good stress provides us with the stimulation, challenge, and energy necessary to pursue our goals and development.

Bad stress makes us anxious and irritable. It is the reaction to known or perceived danger. It is our response to pressure. Our response causes physiological or psychological changes in our attitudes or behaviors. Bad stress or distress is a serious threat to our health. People react differently to circumstances. The same stimulus might trigger different reactions in different people. The circumstance that stresses one person may not ruffle someone else. Hans Seyle, who is called "the father of stress," observes that it is "not the event but your perception of it that makes all the difference."

Stress Peculiar to Women

Today's woman faces multiple causes of stress. This includes taking care of the children, meeting deadlines, dealing with a husband, and working outside of the home. Randy and Nancy Alcorn list a number of stressors that a woman faces:

"Today's mother of school-age children needs the tactical skills of a field marshall. She must get Jimmy ready for school by 8:00 a.m. and be on call in case the carpool driver is ill or can't get her car started. Daughter Jenny goes to a different school that starts at 8:30, but her bus comes at 7:45. Johnny goes to Jenny's school, but he's home at the same time every day (except last week during swimming lessons). . . . Add husband Chuck's erratic work schedule, and you have more variables than a physics equation." (19)

Although this is just a minor part of Mom's schedule, it is a dizzying picture. Many women also have to deal with secondhand stress. This is the stress associated with their husbands' and children's experiences. This is a very true picture of the minister's wife. She often absorbs the problems that affect her husband. This puts a great strain on her. In the face of this strain, the pastor's wife traditionally strives to mask her stress and strain. She smiles at parishioners and demonstrates patience and understanding. She sometimes is forced to entertain—while she is on the verge of screaming, "Would someone help me to run away?" If she has a baby or a couple of toddlers, she is a prime candidate for a breakdown.

Emilie Barnes, in *Survival for Busy Women*, gives a recipe for stress which depicts the lives of most women:

- *3 pounds of Hassles.* Any of life's pressures or traumas will do.
- *5 cups of Hustle.* These are common everyday demands and can be supplied by any family member, neighbor, employer, children's club, church duty, or committee responsibility.
- *7 tablespoons of Hurrieds.* You can pick them fresh, directly off your schedule, expectations, and responsibilities.

  Now stir them up and cook the mixture in the oven of life's trials. Hassled, Hustled, and Hurried—it's a fail-safe formula for a massive serving of stress. Serves one for 24 hours a day, seven days a week, 52 weeks a year. Unless spoiled by organization (20).

One of the chief reasons for stress is lack of organization. Any woman who cares to survive needs a measure of organization. I found that organization was a major way for me to keep my sanity. With a job outside of the home, a busy pastoral husband, and four children, I had to find a way to survive. Lists, family meetings, highlighters on calendars, all kinds of schedules, Post-It notes, and magnets served me well. Shoe boxes, trash bags, baskets, trays, and weekly menu planners were a boon to me. I used any means to help me get organized. Some well-worn mottoes like "Put away, don't put down," and "A place for everything and everything in its place" helped us find our way around the house in peace and safety. So try a plan for organizing your life. It will reduce your stress. You will enjoy a happier home, and you will love it.

Types of Stress Faced by the Pastoral Family
The pastoral family faces multiple types of stress. Some of these stresses are common to other professions as well. However, while some of these stressors are faced by others, it seems as if the ministerial family is plagued by the accumulation of them. Here are a few of the stressors that McBurney lists:

- *Impossible tasks.* The expectations are vastly unreasonable.

- *Mandate to succeed.* One aspect of ministry that sets it apart from other jobs is the sense of "calling" that clergy feel. . . . If God called me to be a pastor, why aren't things going better in my life?
- *Financial pressure.* They are underpaid and yet expected to live up to the lifestyle of their congregations.
- *Cross-cultural adjustment.* Most foreign missionaries are faced with the challenge of learning to live successfully in another culture. (56-65)

This is only a fraction of the stressors that pastoral families experience. We can add problems of family adjustment to the parish, frequent moves, loss of privacy, the social adjustment of the children, conflicts with colleagues, and the general feeling of not being totally accepted because the family are foreigners.

Signs of stress

It is possible to be stressed and not even realize it until someone points it out to you. I remember when our first daughter was preparing to leave home for college. I found myself irritable and teary. I was short-tempered and impatient. This was not me. I felt like a stranger had been released inside of me. One evening I told my husband I could not understand what was going on. Why was I this way? "Oh, you are just stressed because Karen-Mae (our daughter) will be leaving home in a few days" was his calm reply. I was shocked by that diagnosis. I almost felt angry at him for his insight. *Why was I the only one in this situation? Why was he not behaving this way? Wasn't she his daughter, too?* I dissolved into tears. The torrents of tears that had refused to rush down my face before were now released. I had not recognized these signs of stress before.

For years I was terrified of flying. Whenever I had to take a plane, I was in agony for weeks before. I had many sleepless nights, and my fertile imagination worked overtime. What if the plane . . . ? I found that I would be impatient and snap at anyone who lingered in my path. The thought of flying stressed me. My stress was so obvious to my family that our 10-year-old daughter Nelita wrote me a comforting note reminding me that I was in God's care. I kept that note in my passport for more than a decade. I thank God that I am doing so much better now. It is a miracle! I have a "flying job," and God has calmed my nerves tremendously.

Our stressors and our responses to stress are unique to us. What stresses me may pass unnoticed by another. When we recognize the sources of our stress, and the signs are apparent to us, we are better able to deal with them and to control our reactions. Davidson gives four categories of stress:

Anticipatory stress is stress caused by concern over the future.

Situational stress is stress of the moment.

Chronic stress is stress over time.

Residual stress is stress of the past. (19, 20)

How can we recognize the signs of stress? Here are a few common manifestations:

- Dry mouth
- Intestinal distress
- Heavy, short breathing
- Frequent yawning
- Feelings of persistent fatigue
- Clammy, sticky palms
- Irritability
- Craving for sweets
- Lack of concentration
- Combative behavior
- Placing undue emphasis on minutia
- Nail biting
- Tapping feet incessantly
- Feelings of carelessness or recklessness
- Headaches or other body pains

It is amazing how stress can control how we feel and function. Once we recognize the signs or symptoms, we can then deal with the stress.

Sources of stress

There are multiple sources of stress. Stressors can include traffic jams, a long line at the supermarket, a persistent telemarketer, a flat tire when you are late, an approaching deadline, or an impatient and driven boss. Think of the many situations in which you might find yourself, and there we will find an equal number of stressors. Stressors can be categorized into several groups including emotional, familial, social, chemical, job-related, and physical. Each set of stressors has demands and pressures that place wear and tear on our minds and bodies.

Once we identify the source of our stress, we are on the way to coping with it. Not knowing the source of our stress leads to ambivalence and an inability to cope with the pressure. We need to find the stressor and work from that point. Some stressors can be tolerated while others must be eliminated immediately. If one of our coworkers is a whiner or complainer, we can learn to co-exist with that person by planning a coping strategy. Perhaps we may turn a deaf ear to the negativity. If, however, one of our coworkers smokes and spends their lunch break smoking in the employees lounge while we are having lunch, we can eliminate that stressor. We can choose to have a different lunch time or eat our lunch someplace else.

One of the pressures that a pastor's wife bears is that of wearing many hats. We are homemakers, workers outside of the home, taxi drivers, and caregivers at home and in the community. Then we begin to feel and function like Superwoman. Randy and Nanci Alcom describe the superwoman:

"Wherever they go—at home or at the office—these women are constantly giving out for the good of others, giving out but not taking in. Reservoirs drained, they live to please others but have nothing left of themselves. . . . Whether they work outside the home or not, it's no wonder today's women are under stress." (24, 25)

I Think My Husband Stresses Me

The other day, after a discussion with some pastoral wives, I compiled a list of ways in which wives feel stressed—unintentionally, of course—by their husbands. Here is a list of concerns I collected:

- I do not get enough advance notice when we have to meet an appointment.
- He does not offer to help me get the kids ready.
- I get scant information when we are going to an event: What is the dress code? Who else will be there? Will I be expected to do anything? I would like answers to these questions.
- He does not pay attention to how I look; he is only interested in my getting to the event on time.

- He expects me to have everything in order.
- He wants me to do a lot of things at church, in spite of the fact that we have very young children, and my health is fragile. He thinks that is my role, and I will be OK.
- He does not notice when I do not feel well.
- When we go to events, I have to take care of the children all the time while he and his friends get to socialize unencumbered.
- Keeping up with all of the commitments makes me stressed. I need some time out.
- He is always so "busy" that we can hardly get to go grocery shopping or spend time together.
- Getting him to pray with me for my own needs is like pulling teeth.
- He refuses to take care of his health.
- I need to know our financial plans for the future.
- I need to be able to discuss my own goals with him.
- I believe he loves me, but he treats the church members better than he treats me.
- I feel like a stranger in the parsonage. I am clueless about his ministry.
- Sometimes I need for us to laugh and play together.
- My husband does not take me seriously when I tell him how stressed I am.
- I lack affirmation from him.
- I wish he would help me more with the children. I need help nurturing them.

We must not believe that these stressors are deliberately created by pastoral husbands to torment their wives. Here is where communication plays a major role. If there are things that worry you, communicate these to your husband. The only fair thing to do is let your spouse know what hurts, annoys, or generally stresses you. He may be blissfully unaware of your pain. We women tend to mask our pain. Pick an opportune moment to discuss your feelings.

Limit your list of concerns. Do not overwhelm him with too many concerns at once. Pick something that is really important to you and talk about it. Begin your little chat by affirming him about what you are pleased about. Your husband needs to be reminded of his positive points. Commend his strengths.

Let him know how much you appreciate what he does for you and the family.

We all like affirmation. Here are some commendable points that pastors' wives shared about their husbands. Some of these qualities may be on the list you have for your husband:

- My husband calls me to let me know when he will be late for meals.
- Whenever he goes on a trip, my husband calls me regularly.
- My husband never forgets my birthday or our anniversary.
- He likes to shop for me.
- I am in school, and my husband does the cooking.
- He still brings me flowers.
- When I am pregnant, my husband takes excellent care of me.
- He encourages me to have friends.
- He makes me feel special.
- We hold hands in public.
- He helps me achieve my goals.
- I am a stay-at-home wife, and he makes certain I have a bit of money to spend.
- He is a man of integrity.
- We pray together.
- He helps me with the kids.
- He is very careful in his relationships with women.
- I know that he is faithful to me.

With a spirit of calmness and fairness, discuss what bothers you. Then pray about your concerns. If you discover that you and your husband cannot work things out by yourselves, do not be reluctant to get professional help. In the meantime, keep talking to God. He is the greatest stress reliever.

Some Effective Ways of Dealing with Stress

There are multiple ways of dealing with stress. Much depends on the stress-or and the stressed. Some solutions need to be custom-made. *Exercise* and *diet* play significant roles in helping one to deal with stress. Exercise and proper diet will reduce excess fat. "Excess fat means excess physical stress—more strain on your heart, muscles, and bones. Aerobic exercise will reduce excess fat . . . and in the process, excess stress," says Alcorn. (171)

109

After identifying the stressor, one may need to *accept* the situation. Bullying for change increases the stress. It can be frustrating to try to change people. If we fail, we feel disillusioned. We then will need to redirect our goals. Sometimes the need to change does not lie in our environment or in others but in us. Here the Serenity Prayer ("God grant me the serenity to accept the things I cannot change") may be a good motto.

Another method is to *adapt.* There is freedom in flexibility. A rigid approach is sometimes suffocating and uncomfortable. We may have our ideals, but the existing circumstances may not allow us to realize those ideals. The pastor's wife may dream of teaching the kindergarten class at church. However, because she has two toddlers of her own, her plate may be too full to allow her to prepare teaching aids and plan lessons. Instead of allowing this situation to stress her, the ministerial wife may adjust her dream for serving at church until her toddlers have grown older, or she may choose another area of service in the meantime. Adapting is another way of dealing with stress.

Being in control of a situation is another effective way of dealing with stress. When we have lost control, we tend to suffer from high levels of stress. What are we to control? We are to control our anger, our fears, and our goals. Are we going to allow people or situations to anger us? Will our fears master us? Will we move toward our goals or will we be drifters? We do not usually lose control. What happens is that we give up our control. We need to control our mindset and our direction. Being in control gives us strength to cope and move on.

It is amazing how many little things take control of us: the telephone, an unexpected visitor, the movie that surprised us with an explicit scene, a sudden change in a meeting place. These are things that can wrest control from us— but only if we surrender that control. We must not allow things that threaten to control us, to stress us.

Take a Break Sometimes

"What is life if full of care / We have no time to stand and stare?"

Have you ever felt like a spinning top? Sometimes just looking at my to-do list makes me dizzy. We either feel guilty doing nothing or we do something to keep from feeling guilty. I have heard myself say many times, "I had a really productive day today. I got a lot done." Why does one have to accomplish a lot in order to be productive? What is wrong with getting only a few things done but being able to "stand and stare"? Somebody made us feel that non-activity is sinful. I remember my teachers in elementary school saying to our class, "The devil finds work for idle hands to do." Now we believe that resting hands are "idle hands," and the devil will soon be employing us. So we make a frenzied dash to keep the devil away.

We can also get stressed from too much activity. Over-commitment and crowded schedules contribute to our stress. We are not singing the praises of laziness. The wise man Solomon utters many derogatory statements about the lazy person. He praises the industriousness of the simple ant and recommends her as a model of wisdom. That is a staggering compliment from the wisest man who ever lived. However, in the midst of our engagements, demands, and deadlines, we must pause sometimes.

Mr. Jones, an elderly man, lay on his hospital bed, weak from a recent serious illness. Dolly, a sprightly neighbor, went to visit him. After a few initial questions about the man's health and a brief update on the news of their neighborhood, Dolly set to work. She pulled the blinds and gave a quick commentary on the activities in the street below. Next, she checked the patient's flask to see if it needed refilling. She turned the man, first to the left and then to the right, as she contrived to fluff his pillows for him. The poor man groaned from the discomfort that came about because of the movement. He was becoming exhausted as his eyes followed his flitting, well-meaning neighbor. Too bad he lacked the strength to shackle her into a stationary position!

Meanwhile, Dolly surveyed the room with questioning eyes. Then she ventured, "What else may I do for you, Mr. Jones?"

"Nothing, thanks, Dolly. Don't do something, just stand there."

Many times we think that we have to always be doing something, but this is not true. Jesus encouraged us to rest. A friend of mine says, "Rest is legal." We can sit or stand and just do nothing. In the Bible, Martha was very busy fixing dinner for Jesus and His disciples. I picture her moving at lightning speed, firing multiple, sometimes unintelligible orders to her servants. A tempest of thoughts raced through Martha's mind. *Why in the world would my sister Mary not be sensitive enough to enter this kitchen and lend a hand?* Mary was not in the kitchen. Mary was listening to Jesus. Imagine Martha's disgust! Here she was working her fingers to the bone, and was Mary helping her? No. Mary "sat at Jesus' feet and heard his word" (Luke 10:39).

Martha complained to Jesus. But Jesus did not send Mary to the kitchen with explicit orders to help her sister. In fact, it was Martha to whom Jesus gave a mild reprimand. "Martha, Martha, thou art careful and troubled about many things" (Luke 10:41). Jesus was quite pleased that Mary "sat." It is by sitting or standing still that we are able to hear the voice of Jesus. Hustle and bustle drown out the voice of our Lord. "Be still and know that I am God" (Ps. 46:10). A time-out from activity helps us connect with God. We need that connection.

Slow down. Stop. Enjoy the smell of a rose. Hear the crashing of the waves. Feel the breeze on your face. Smile at a kid. Marvel at a rainbow. It's OK sometimes to just stand there and do nothing. It can reduce your stress.

Turn It Over to God

After we have worked at dealing with stress, the most important step is to *turn our stress over to God.* We have a heavenly Father who is ready to accept our stressors and our stress. I like this invitation: "Casting all your care upon him; for he careth for you" (1 Peter 5:7). The great, wonderful God who's "got the whole world in His hands" can relieve you of your stress and fill your heart and mind with His peace.

CHAPTER 11

IT'S OK TO LAUGH

Some people never laugh. In fact, I know some people who barely smile. I don't think that they have resolved to have sour countenances; smiles and laughter just aren't on their agenda. These people are naturally very serious in appearance. They are not unpleasant, but they do not laugh nor smile. If only they knew the enhancing power of a smile! Others smile easily and have a ready sense of humor. I like people who can laugh and enjoy a clean joke. A good belly-shaking exercise has benefits for all of us.

Many years ago, I attended a national music festival. Several male groups participated, and the quality of their voices was superb. Their tones were mellow and the harmony was pleasing to the ear. There is something special about the blend of rich male voices.

The lyrics of the song, which was the test piece for the competitors, described a beautiful young lady who was being wooed by love-sick suitor. There was a high standard of performance. Soon the winners of the competition were announced. The gasp of disappointment that followed the judges' announcement indicated that the runners-up seemed to have been the popular choice of the crowd. Many seemed to believe that these second-place singers had better voice quality, smoother tones, and an overall more professional appearance. However, the judges' comments were revealing. The judges noted that in spite of the superior voice quality and professional presentation of the runners-up, they could not be the winners because the expressions on their faces were too serious and lacked the warmth and tenderness of lovers. "How could you woo a young lady and hope to win her without a smile on your face?" declared the leader of the panel of judges.

I often ask myself a similar question. *How can one be really nice to be around if no smiles are allowed to escape, at least occasionally?*

To Laugh or Not to Laugh

Laughter is biblical. The wise man Solomon declared that there is "a time to laugh" (Eccl. 3:4). In Job 8:21 we read of God filling our mouths with laughter. "He will fill your mouth with laughter and your lips with shouts of joy." We can therefore have no doubt that laughter *is* a gift from God. Who has not been charmed by the bell-like sounds of children's laughter ringing through the air and warming our hearts? There is something almost magical about laughter and smiles. They are universal, eloquent, and infectious.

No Barriers

The other day I was sitting beside a Russian lady at a conference. She spoke no English, and I cannot speak Russian. There was no one else within about three feet of either of us. I dreaded the potentially mandatory silence. "Habla español?" I ventured. Why I concluded that a Russian lady would be speaking Spanish is beyond me! Anyway, she responded with a negative nod. I was determined to assure my seatmate that I was a friendly, non-threatening sister, so I simply looked at her and smiled. She responded in a similar fashion. From then on we punctuated our glances with mutual smiles. I wondered what we would have done without the medium of a smile.

The Gift

Smiles and laughter can reduce or even banish boredom and monotony. Many of us have heard that it takes more facial muscles to frown than to smile. Then it is not such a bad idea to consider that by reducing the wear and tear on our facial muscles, we can hold back the threatening wrinkles.

A sense of humor in a family is like a breath of fresh air. It is like opening a window, pulling the shades, and letting the sunshine in. A sense of humor is not a natural endowment for all of us, but a measure of it can be cultivated. We are not talking about gross or offensive humor here. It is unacceptable to laugh when someone gets hurt or suffers embarrassment. However, we should try to find the funny side of things sometimes and even laugh at ourselves. Laughter helps to lighten the load. Pastors' wives need to develop and appreciate a sense of humor. Laughing heartily and enjoying a side-splitting joke can be revitalizing. Our lives are so full of stress and the challenges are so weighty that a detour down Comedy Lane is sometimes welcome.

My husband Jansen and I both have a sense of humor. It is one of those genetic gifts from both sides of our families. Our four children have inherited this also. Now I am beginning to observe traces of this precious gift in our grandchildren. That makes me very happy.

Jansen and I had been married for about six months when an older pastor's wife met us in a little town. "Hello, my dear Brother. Hello, my dear Sister," declared Sister in her you-youngsters-had-better-realize-that ministry-is-serious-business voice. "And how are you today?"

"Very well, thanks," we responded in a feeble duet. Something inside of me did not feel enthusiastic about this woman. I had nightmares of having to explain to this veteran pastor's wife the doctrine of the 2,300-day prophecy of Daniel 8 in order to prove my eligibility for being a minister's wife.

"Well, Brother," said she, directing her attention to Jansen, "how is married life treating you?"

"Well," replied Jansen with his characteristic mischievous grin, "I'm trying to keep up with the hard times."

Big mistake! This was no place for Jansen's humor.

"Hard times! What hard times?"

"Well, it is this wife of mine," continued my dear husband, totally unaware of his danger. "We have this problem . . . " And the danger continues.

"Problem? What problem, Brother? A problem with your wife?" She urged him on. This was going to be an opportunity for her to teach this young 20-something wife a thing or two. I could almost feel her judgmental claws closing in on my neck.

"This wife of mine is not feeding me well. She cooks the same food every day, and I have to eat it," offered Jansen, still woefully oblivious to his impending peril—*my* peril!

Before this incident, I had suspected that men lack intuition. Now I had no doubts. My husband did not know that some people find humor sinful and take life seriously all the time. His brilliant male mind did not reveal to him that this lady had no time to be funny and frivolous, that her purpose in life was to drag souls into the Kingdom of God, that she believed that life was no laughing matter. So my dear husband proceeded down the path to destruction—my destruction.

Our friend pulled herself up to her full stature and proceeded to impress upon me my need to learn good nutrition and to "feed the elder well. You can't do that, Sister. Elder here needs good nutrition. You gotta do better than that. You gotta do better than that."

By this time, I was cringing under her self-righteous, insensitive blows and incisive claws. I was unable to dodge them; I just had to endure them. Meanwhile, Jansen was trying to convince the lady that he was not serious. Despite this, he sounded like an evangelist making a futile altar call. He fought hard to convert her to thinking that he had this sense of humor that just popped out at times. But nothing worked. He looked helplessly at me. He felt hurt for me.

The pastor's wife clung tenaciously to her little refrain: "You gotta do better than that, Sister."

Really funny

How boring it must be to be so permanently serious, so unbearably correct, and so devoid of fun and laughter! Our library at home boasts a number of books about humor. They range from military humor to humor in church to humorous toasts and even humorous newspaper announcements. When our children were young and their dad wanted to treat them to a video, the kids would roam the aisles of videos in the store, reminding their dad, "Daddy, let's see what we can find to make Mommy laugh."

Sharon Cress, Associate Secretary of the General Conference Ministerial Association and the coordinator of the Ministry to Clergy Spouses, has published a book for pastor's wives. *Seasoned with Laughter* is a book full of tear-jerking, spleen-splitting jokes gleaned from parsonages around the world. Here are a few samples of some really funny pastoral jokes:

*****

"In the region of Ukraine where we live, inflation is always high. Apparently, my conversations with my husband about how high prices were climbing and how we would survive made an impression on our four-year-old daughter, Lillia. One day she asked, 'Mommy, will you buy me a dress?' I explained that she already had a dress and did not need another one. 'But I need a wedding dress!' she insisted. 'Why do you need a wedding dress?' I inquired. 'Because when I am old enough to get married, the prices will be so high, we won't be able to afford one!' "—Anna Kuzmitch, Ukraine (85)

*****

"One Sabbath morning, my son saw me trim a stray hair from my chin. Later on, when it was time for prayer requests at church, he called out, 'You need to pray for my Mommy because she is turning into a man like my Daddy!'"—Bernie Holford, England (44).

*****

"For Friday night Consecration service, I came into the church and, greeting members along the way, walked to the front row. When I sat down, a gentleman behind me said loudly, "The administrator's wife dresses with etiquette!" I turned around and smiled, thinking he was complementing me on my dress. A few minutes later, I heard him say it again. Finally, another lady came up and told me the designer tag on the back of my dress was hanging out. I was mortified because in Spanish, 'etiquette' means nicely dressed, but it also means the tag of the garment!"— Edilma de Poloche, Venezuela (64)

*****

I have had my own humorous experiences when the tears of laughter streamed down my face. One of the most trying circumstances for me is when something funny happens in church and I am supposed to be serious and professional. Then I find myself employing all kinds of ways to suppress my laughter. I remember one day at church when the sermon was rather lengthy. Our little three-year-old was becoming restless. There was a rapid succession of questions: "Do you think church is almost over? When are we going home?" Then came the dreaded pronouncement, "Mommy, I am hungry. I want to go home." Every mother breaks out into a nervous sweat when a little one makes such a statement in church. Mothers interpret this as *if you do not do something about my famished state NOW, I will make life unbearable for you!!!!*

I realized that the preacher was wrapping up his sermon, or at least I hoped so. I coaxed my child for a bit and thought that since she had no more interest in coloring, we would play a little game in the pew. I said to her, "Sweetie, let us just keep our eyes on the preacher and with our fingers do whatever he does. If he waves his arms, we will wave our fingers. When he hits the desk, we will tap on the pew with our fingers, and so on. But, you see, we really have to look at him very carefully."

Well, that seemed to work for a precious three or so minutes, and I was beginning to feel very proud of my creativity. Then, all of a sudden, our daughter blurted out in full volume, "Mommeeee, don't you think that preacher looks like the devil?" Instinctively I turned to look behind to see if there had been any damage. For several rows behind us, there were people shaking convulsively with suppressed laughter.

Well, it is OK for pastors' wives to laugh. Try it. You'll like it.

Molly Detweiler presents the importance of laughter in *Laughter for a Woman's Soul*: "A laugh lifestyle is predicated upon our attitude toward the daily stuff of life. When those tasks seem too dull to endure, figure out a way to make them fun, get creative, and entertain yourself. . . . Find something in the midst of the pain that makes you smile or giggle anyway. There's always something somewhere . . . even if you have to pretend to laugh until you really do!" (65)

A Good Medicine

"A merry heart doeth good like a medicine: but a broken spirit drieth the bones" (Prov. 17:22). Who wants dry bones? Dry bones are brittle and break. Women over 30 are especially subject to brittle bones. Broken bones often cause falls or at least reduced mobility. Our movements are restricted, and we are not very happy on crutches or in bandages or casts. Laughter is a necessary medicine for us.

Let us ponder another translation of Proverbs 17:22. "A cheerful disposition is good for your health; gloom and doom leave you bone-tired" (*The Message*). Cheerfulness is a wonderful gift that others can enjoy. When we think of what Jesus has done for us by giving us eternal life, how can we be gloomy? We need to let the sunshine of God's love into our hearts. John Wesley once said, "Sour godliness is the devil's religion."

One way to develop a cheerful spirit is by praising God. The psalmist revealed, "Our mouths were filled with laughter, our tongues with songs of joy. Then it was said among the nations, 'The Lord has done great things for them' " (Ps. 126:2). What an eloquent witness our cheerful spirits can be! Praise God continually. I cannot help repeating how much I like Psalm 119:164: "Seven times a day will I praise thee because of thy righteous judgment." Try this daily quota of praise. It works.

Think about what a broken spirit or sad heart does to our relationships. We women are the "tone-setters" in our homes. Sometimes we allow the cares of life to suffocate us so that the sunshine of laughter is absent. I remember teaching our girls a song that went like this:

So let the sun shine in, face it with a grin,
Smilers never lose and frowners never win.
So let the sun shine in, face it with a grin.
Open up your heart and let the sun shine in.

When we allow laughter to enter our homes, stress and pain do not have as much of a hold on us. "Laughter is an incredible gift. It helps us not to take ourselves too seriously and makes it possible for us to survive life's awkward moments," says humorist Patsy Clairmont in her book *Normal is Just a Setting on Your Dryer.* (48)

Of greater importance is what a gloomy spirit does to our own health. There has been much emphasis in recent times on laughter and the state of our health. Norman Cousins, author of *Anatomy of an Illness,* discovered that he had a painful, crippling disease. In order to be comfortable for short periods each day, Cousins was given very potent painkillers and anti-inflammatory medications that promised to have serious long-term side effects. This was not acceptable to him, so he decided to move out of the hospital. He stopped the medications, took massive doses of vitamin C, and hired a private nurse who read many humorous stories to him daily. Also, Cousins viewed several funny films every day. His health improved notably. Cousins does not attribute his improved health to laughter alone, but he maintains that positive emotions can have a healing effect and can aid in combating disease. There has been much research undertaken to uncover the chemical changes that take place in our bodies to reduce pain and relieve stress. Laughter is good for our health. It is no wonder that this little saying has become popular: "A laugh a day keeps the doctor away."

Try It

You may ask, "What if there is nothing to laugh about? I don't even feel like smiling." Sometimes life's pressures are so heavy that there seems to be no room for smiles and laughter. Yet you do not have to be always gloomy and sad.

If you find yourself constantly teary and heavy-hearted, visit your doctor. That is a good place to start.

Happiness is a choice, so choose to be happy and cheerful. Happiness is God's plan for you. He wants you to laugh and be happy. Think of all of His blessings. Think of what He has saved you from. Praise Him. Shout "Hallelujah!" Sing songs of praise and thankfulness.

The other day I was reading a delightful little volume, *Laughter is the Spice of Life,* when I came across an excerpt from *Traveler's Gift*: "Today I will choose to be happy. I will greet each day with laughter. Within moments of awakening, I will laugh for seven seconds. Even after such a small period of time, excitement has begun to flow through my bloodstream. . . . I will greet each day with laughter. . . . Today, I will choose to be happy." (5-6)

Trust Jesus to put the laughter back into your life. "Jesus said, 'Blessed are you who weep now, for you will laugh' " (Luke 6:21, NIV). This is what He wants for you. All you need to do is claim His precious promises. "He will fill your mouth with laughter and your lips with shouts of joy" (Job 8:21, NIV).

CHAPTER 12

THE SKY IS YOUR LIMIT

I am afraid of heights. My vivid imagination finds ways of conjuring up all kinds of deadly possibilities when I am more than eight feet above the ground. Yet I am fascinated by the miniature cars and buildings that I see when I dare to look down from a high tower. Perhaps my acrophobia is only borderline.

This chapter is about heights—the heights that God expects us to reach. What I like about God is that His expectations for us are realistic. Our responsibility is not to limit ourselves. "You may every one of you make your mark. You should be content with no mean attainments. Aim high and spare no pains to reach the standard" (*Messages to Young People*, 36). These words of Ellen G. White are a strong motivation for us to reach for the stars.

When I was a kid in high school, our principal often gave us powerful motivational capsules during our morning assemblies. He hammered into our ears the importance of not being satisfied with mediocrity. He said that there was such an overabundance of mediocre people in this world, that there is much room at the top for excellence. That concept impressed me. Then later I came across a poster that read "Aim at the stars and you can't shoot lower than the trees." I recall sharing these thoughts with my own students in high school when I became an English teacher.

Will the Good Fairy Come?

When we were children, we heard stories of people who were in unfortunate circumstances until a good fairy came along and waved a wand. Then the people's luck changed instantly. There was Cinderella whose smoky tatters were transformed into a stunning princess's gown at the wave of a fairy godmother's wand. Cinderella was whisked from poverty to a palace. Quantum leaps to wealth and fame were possible in fairy tales. However, in real life, success is spelled in terms of hard work and determination.

Of course there have been real people who have, in spite of dire circumstances, attained fame, wealth, and happiness. We are inspired by people of humble beginnings who became success stories. Think of Abraham Lincoln, born in a log cabin. His family was poor, but he had such a consuming passion for learning that he would walk miles to borrow a book. He also made the journey back to return the books he borrowed. His determination to become somebody directed his dream until he reached the White House as the sixteenth President of the United States. There was also the late President Gerald Ford, who started life as an abandoned baby. Ford became the thirty-eighth President of the United States. We are also awed by generous donors who spent their childhood in poverty but who now, because of the wealth they acquired, are able to make huge contributions to various charities. We are thankful for these persons who are committed to giving the less fortunate a better life.

Other people have been able to pursue their dreams successfully because their beginnings were advantageous. They were born into families with money. They lived in communities where education was encouraged. Opportunities seemed to present themselves to these people. We say they had good beginnings in their favor.

What constitutes a good beginning? Is it possible to secure a good beginning? The best guarantee for a good beginning is a beginning with God. Rely on the word, "In the beginning God . . ." (Gen. 1:1). Every day is a new beginning with new opportunities. We need not wait for a new year to experience a new beginning. That is the problem with many of us; we confine our opportunities for new beginnings to the calendar. *On January 1, I will begin my exercise program. I will commit to my daily private devotions. I will read a portion of a good book daily. I will smile at my family. I will choose not to let anyone make me ugly. I will* . . . By January 27 we find ourselves reneging on our resolutions. That discourages us. This is not good for us. If we fall on January 27, we can rise again and continue the race on January 28. God's opportunities are new every morning.

New Things

The other day, I received a note from a young lady. I was thrilled by her statement: "I am new." I thought that that was a beautiful conviction. We all like new things: new homes, new cars, new clothes, new years, and even new acquaintances. Sometimes we are tempted to "forsake the old for the new." The other day I heard of a man who deserted his wife of 30 years. He said she was too old, and he wanted a new wife. How sad! Let's hope that this man's "new" wife was excited about the *old* husband she was getting.

It is fine to like new things. God likes new things. He offers us a new heart. His Word urges us to put on the "new man." We are advised to walk in "newness of life." He gave us a new commandment to love one another. We are promised a "new heaven and a new earth." When we get to heaven, we will get new names.

If we depend on God, He will give us the new things we need—energy, goals, wisdom, and a new brand of determination to reach for the stars. Let us claim God's promise in Isaiah 43:19: "Behold, I will do a new thing. Now it shall spring forth; shall ye not know it? I will even make a way in the wilderness and rivers in the desert."

Goals, Goals

Times moves relentlessly on, and if we do not plan our lives, we will find ourselves drifting aimlessly. So many things seem to have happened "just yesterday." How time flies! It is very easy for a wife to fall into a routine of taking care of her family, the church, and the community to the exclusion of fulfilling her personal goals. Some women articulate their goals early in life and pursue them. Others are late bloomers. There are different reasons for this. Perhaps the wife was giving her husband the first chance at getting his education and career off the ground. It could be that she wanted to devote her time to taking care of their young children. Plans may have been interrupted by illness or limited funds. A desire to change her career or frequent pastoral moves could have been contributing factors to the delayed achievement of goals of the pastor's wife. These are all legitimate reasons. However, there comes a time to set some goals and to decide on a plan of action.

A woman must resist circumstances or people who tend to divert her from her goals. There are times when we may have to delay our dreams, but there must also come the time to resume the pursuit of those dreams. Our goals belong to us. Nobody should be allowed to dilute the strength of our ambitions. God is willing to unite with us in our quest for a brighter future. "For I know the plans I have for you, plans to prosper you and not to harm you; plans to give you hope and a future" (Jer. 29:11). Bitterness and resentment can result from unfulfilled dreams. There is hardly one who at some time has not felt the desire to do something grand or to make a contribution to society or to the family. When that desire is squelched, we feel deflated and our spirits droop. How can we view the sky as our limit when we can barely spy our earthly goal? What can we do to reach those elusive goals?

In her book *You Matter More Than You Think,* Leslie Parrot shares a compelling personal experience. She says that it was not until someone urged her to talk about her dreams that she started really thinking about them. "Here is what I dream of doing over the next ten years," was her reply. "And I slid my yellow pad of paper across his desk. On the pad was a list of five sentences: I want to earn my doctorate. I want to run the L.A. Marathon. I want to have three children. I want to write children's books. I want to teach and mentor college students." (69)

Leslie Parrot confessed that she would never have been definitive about her dreams if she had not been forced into the situation. "I probably would not have even thought much further than getting my husband through school, having a home, and raising a family. . . . Though I never would have believed it at the time, writing down my dreams helped me to realize all but one of them. I had just two children, not three." (69)

So, my dear sister, get a dream. Dream big and then move in that direction!

The first step is to place your goals before God. We have already established that our plans must begin with God. With God in the beginning, we cannot help but get wisdom. "The fear of the Lord is the beginning of wisdom." Right at the beginning, Solomon asked God for wisdom. He got it.

God's Word invites us to seek wisdom from God. "If you want to know what God wants you to know, ask Him and He will gladly tell you" (James 1:5, LB). Seek God's pleasure in your plans. Ask Him to walk you through your journey.

The second step is to stay focused on your goals. Now that you have articulated your goals, where do you want to go? What do you want from life? Where

WHAT NO ONE TELLS THE PASTOR'S WIFE

do you expect to be in the next two years, or five years, or even ten years? By adding passion to your goals, you will find yourself able to forge ahead in spite of obstacles. Do not be discouraged by hindrances. Realize that with God, your possibilities are limitless and your goals are reachable. Ellen White says, "You have within your reach more than finite possibilities" (*Messages to Young People*, 47). Let your goals be lofty, not microscopic. The God of your goals is mighty, abundant, and awesome.

The third step is to work hard. A Gallup poll conducted extensive research on the qualities of success. The pollsters spent thousands of hours interviewing successful people in all areas of life—the military, business, the arts, religion, and so on. They discovered that the common denominator was not a lucky break, extraordinary talent, shortcuts, or even wealth. It was hard work! All of the people who were interviewed attributed their success to hard work. Hard work and determination are an unbeatable combination. Work hard, persevere, and hold on to your spirit of determination. One cannot work hard on and off. Consistency is necessary. Note what this anonymous author says about perseverance and determination:

> "Press on. Nothing in the world can take the place of persistence. Talent will not; nothing is more common than unsuccessful men with talent. Genius will not; unrewarded genius is almost a proverb. Education will not; the world is full of educated derelicts. Persistence and determination alone are important."

The fourth step is to consider the importance of relationships. Choosing our associations with care is of utmost importance. Sometimes our friends influence us to short-circuit our goals. Some people are not interested in our progress. Still others do not have faith in our abilities to succeed, and they discourage us. We need to keep close to us those who are ambitious for us and who will support us in our goals. We also need to be close to those who are committed to a relationship with Jesus. In Proverbs 1:10, Solomon gives us a major qualification of the type of relationship we should cherish: "If sinners entice thee, consent thou not."

When we think of relationships, we sometimes minimize our contribution to healthy relationships. We should be kind and generous. We should do good deeds for others and hasten to do it. "Withhold not good from them to whom it is due, when it is in the power of thine hand to do it. Say not unto thy neighbor, go and come again and tomorrow I will give; when thou hast it by thee" (Prov. 3:27, 28). Do it now.

It is unfortunate that in the pursuit of our goals, we sometimes forget the importance of kindness, caring, sharing, and respect for others in our relationships. These must not be lacking. We impress people more with our caring than with our talents.

The fifth step is to ignore the chorus of doomsday singers. Too often there are those who stand by and denounce people's dreams. They shout, "It can't be done. You cannot make it." Instead of being cheerleaders, they are the doomsday chorus. "You are not smart enough. You are attempting too much. Your family needs your support. You cannot afford it." This is the time to put your earplugs in and move on in the assurance that God will see you through. This is no time to listen to despair and prophecies of failure.

Limitations can be a barrier to success. We impose limitations on ourselves, and others impose limitations on us. But we are not in the business of limitations; we are moving on in the march toward success. With God on our side, we will be victorious. Hold on to the following assurance found in *Messages to Young People*: "As the will of man cooperates with the will of God, it becomes omnipotent. . . . All His biddings are enablings." (Ellen G. White, 101)

Realize that success without integrity is empty. We may achieve our dearest dreams and climb to the highest heights, but if our steps are not marked with integrity, we are nothing. According to Karl Haffneck, "You can drive a Corvette, get a degree from Harvard, vacation in Australia, even golf with a handicap . . . but you'll never be truly successful unless everything you do is undergirded with integrity. Only when truthfulness is deeply embedded in your character will you taste the heady portion of success." How profound! We have all seen people who have made gigantic strides economically and educationally, but they have been plummeted into disgrace because of their lack of integrity. The wise man Solomon reminds us of the importance of integrity: "Better is the poor that walketh in his integrity" (Prov. 19:1). A truly successful person is one who enjoys the respect of others because he is honest, transparent, and truthful. Many of us are familiar with the following statement: "The greatest want in the world is the want of men [women]—who will not be bought or sold, men [women] who in their inmost souls are true and honest, men [women] who do not fear to call sin by its right name, men [women] whose conscience is as true to duty as the needle to the pole, men [women] who will stand for the right though the heavens fall." (Ellen G. White, *Education*, 57)

There is Help

Now that we have set our goals and are moving to see our dreams fulfilled, how can we be sure that we will make it to the end? I remember very clearly the 400-meter semi-finals in the 1992 Olympics in Barcelona, Spain. The spotlight was on Derek Redmond. It was this same Redmond who, in 1988 in Seoul, had to withdraw from the Games just 10 minutes before the start of the race because he had sustained an injury to his Achilles tendon. Redmond had undergone a series of surgeries to repair the tendon, and now, four years later, he had another opportunity to compete in the Olympics.

About 65,000 spectators were crammed into the stands, and there was an air of expectancy as the race began. Soon Derek Redmond came into view and forged past the other competitors. The crowd cheered as they saw their favorite gaining ground. Then it happened. In a split second, when he was only 175 meters from the finish line, Redmond heard a pop in his right hamstring. He wobbled and, clutching his leg, fell on the track.

There was silence as the athlete lay almost motionless. He refused to allow the medical personnel to put him on a stretcher. Then, slowly and in obvious pain, Redmond pulled himself up. "Go, go, go," chanted the supportive crowd. "You can make it. Go, go, go."

Encouraged by the chorus of fans, Derek made a gallant attempt. First feebly, then with more courage, he rejoined the race. By this time, many of his competitors were closing in on him. Some shot past him, but Redmond pushed on. Could he make it to the finish line?

Suddenly, in a flash, a middle-aged gentleman leaped from the stands and, defying security, darted to Derek's side. Putting an arm around the young man's waist, he whispered, "I am here; we'll finish together." It was Derek's dad! Together, father and son hobbled toward the finish line. When only a short distance away, his dad released Derek to cross the finish line by himself.

The stands erupted in applause. Amid screaming fans and waving flags, a commentator choked on his tears as he struggled to broadcast the results of the race. This earthly father had helped his son to the finish line.

Would not our heavenly Father do even more? Do not fear that you may not be able to reach the finish line of your goals. I like the *Contemporary English Version* of Philemon 1:6: "God is the one who began this good work in you, and I am certain that he won't stop before it is complete on the day that Christ returns."

So pursue your goals. Be the best you can be. The sky is your limit. I like the following statement in Ellen White's *Education:* "Higher than the highest human thought can reach is God's ideal for His children." (18) What a statement! Pause for a moment and visualize the highest position you can imagine for yourself. What is your loftiest wish? Now believe that God has something greater and grander and better for you. "Higher than the highest human thought can reach." Is that not even higher than the sky?

CHAPTER 13

CAUTION: WOLVES CROSSING

A wolf resembles a dog and is in fact a member of the canine family. A baby wolf is just as cute as a domestic puppy. However, we do not connect with adult wolves in the same way as we do with dogs, although there have been a few stories of children who have been cared for by wolves. One of the earliest Roman legends is that of twin brothers, Romulus and Remus, who were abandoned near the River Tiger. A she-wolf found them and nursed them as her own babies. The city of Rome was allegedly named after Romulus.

Wolves are not necessarily welcome in our society. We feel more comfortable when they restrict their movements to the wild. In fact, we associate despicable traits with wolves. The Apostle Paul expressed his concern about possible attacks on the early Christians. "For I know this, that after my departing shall grievous wolves enter among you, not sparing the flock" (Acts 20:29).

Friends of the Pastor's Wife

It is important for the pastor's wife to be careful about her association with the men and women in the church and the community. As pastors' wives, we encounter people with varying personalities. We must deal with all in a Christ-like manner. We must ask ourselves, "What would Jesus do?" We must never forget that humans are God's creatures, objects of His eternal love made in His image.

There are two main schools of thought regarding socializing in the parish. Some feel that the wife of the pastor should be civil with all but very friendly with none. Others propose that the pastor's wife ought to be the friendliest person on the planet. She must be outgoing and gushing with everyone.

Extremes can be dangerous; the middle of the road seems to be the safest route. Relationships can be critical, and successful relationships require a balance of warmth, caring, discretion, and common sense. A Christian must be unselfish and loving while at the same time being perceptive and wise. In addition, a pastor's wife must be professional.

So must the pastor's wife have friends? Why not? As in any relationship, however, there are necessary guidelines to be followed. Some people are naturally friendly and will gravitate readily to the pastor's wife. They sense her loneliness or her heavy responsibilities and feel a commitment to be her friend. They like her. Then there are others who will keep their distance, not because they do not like her but because they do not want to be accused of pushing themselves into her company. A hint of acceptance from her, though, will encourage them to form friendships with her. Still others who present themselves as friends are not really genuine. They are merely curious about finding out what goes on in the parsonage.

We are social beings. God made a world full of people so that we could choose a few friends to help us enjoy life and share our burdens. We need picnics and parties and other events that will meet our social needs. Association with people can aid our growth as we learn from each other. The challenge lies in balance. Everyone should have the assurance of our acceptance. No one must feel excluded. Yet because we naturally connect with some persons easier than with others, there will be a few who will automatically be a bit closer to us.

What does it mean for some church members to be "closer to us than others"? It means that there might be some common interests shared. Of course barriers are still to be observed. We do not give up our professional garb. We do not surrender our Christian standards. We keep our private lives private. Gossip is taboo. The book of Proverbs is full of advice on relationships. The wise man also warns against frequent visiting in people's homes. "Withdraw thy foot from thy neighbor's house; lest he be weary of thee and so hate thee" (Prov. 25:17).

Get together to strengthen each other spiritually. There are many blessings for us to share. Activities like shopping, exchanging recipes, and engaging in other benign pursuits are recommended. We may even team up with some ladies as missionary partners. The idea is not to initiate an exclusive "Pastor's Wife's Club." The objective is to promote healthy social relationships.

Female Wolves

One needs to be on the lookout for social pitfalls while at the same time not being paranoid. The pastor is often thrown into the company of many types of ladies—efficient, committed, attractive, compassionate, and successful. Many of these ladies are consecrated Christians, but unfortunately, some of them are not. Therefore, there may be feelings of insecurity that plague the wife of the pastor when these ladies are in the pastor's company.

Here are some strategies that can help us protect our husbands while we secure our positions. Be a visible wife. In the eyes of the congregation, your visibility will establish your close relationship with your husband. Your husband does not need a phantom wife. The pastor's wife must be real, near, and visible. Pastors who habitually appear without their wives are in a position to send dangerous signals. Take care of your health and appearance so that you will resist the urge to be frequently absent. All men, including pastors, like attractive wives. Therefore, we women owe it to ourselves to keep ourselves attractive. This is not an excuse for extravagant spending. Our clothes do not have to be showy. We do not need to wear daring styles in an attempt to draw attention to ourselves. All we need to do is take care of how we package ourselves. Modesty, appropriateness, and elegant taste ought to be our guidelines.

Some wives have a strange spirit of self-sacrifice. They are careful to make their husbands and children dress well, but they neglect their own appearance. You may not be able to afford a huge wardrobe, but you certainly owe it to yourself to have a few well-fitting dresses with matching accessories. Shop with care. Browse through catalogs to sharpen your fashion sense. Recognize that current fashions may not be suitable for you. Apart from our responsibility to observe modesty, we need fabrics, fashions, and fit that are becoming to us. If you are blessed with the talent of sewing, celebrate your good fortune. If you are not, it is a good idea to take sewing classes. I am so glad I did. While I did not blossom into a world-class designer, I learned a lot about how to assess and buy fabric and clothing. I can now enter a dress shop with the confidence that I am not going to be at the mercy of the sales attendant. It is important to be a smart buyer. A smart buyer of clothes is not a relentless bargain hunter. A bargain dress that does not flatter your figure is not a bargain, regardless of the price. The smart buyer who has a limited budget purchases clothes that last longer than one year. Make a list of your accessories and choose colors that go with them. Pick fabric that is of good quality. And learn the magic of mixing and matching; you will be amazed at how you will multiply your outfits. Take time with your appearance. With a little planning and imagination, you can look stunning.

We dwell on the packaging, but there is more to beauty than the exterior. Beauty comes from the inside out. Jesus is the Author of loveliness. He is the Bright and Morning Star, the Lily of the Valley, the Altogether Lovely. With Jesus as our close Friend, we have winning chances of being lovely. I praise God for this assurance. It is the entrance of Jesus into our lives and His abiding presence that transform us into beauty queens. I know this idea of beauty appeals to us women, and that is fine. Jesus washes us, cleanses us, clothes us in His righteousness, and what a stunning product He makes us into!

Continuing-education classes and self-improvement projects will help boost our confidence and self-esteem. We were not meant to be mediocre. We must not be reluctant to read and study and improve our skills. Opportunities for improvement are all around us. We must not be left behind. Spend some time finding out what you like to do and what talents you have. God will keep His promise to give us wisdom. "If any of you lacks wisdom, he should ask God, who gives generously to all without finding fault, and it will be given to him" (James 1:5 NIV).

Another point for consideration is the importance of being tactful and mature when dealing with the ladies in the congregation. Guarding your husband like a watch dog is distasteful, suffocating, and uncomfortable for him. He needs his space. Demonstrations of jealousy and suspicion are non-productive and may cause the church members to lose respect for you, and you may also embarrass your husband. This is an ineffective way of protecting our husbands.

Sometimes our intuition may warn us of impending danger from a designing woman or two. Use the gift of your intuition to alert your pastor-husband. Men do not pick up certain signals, and it helps to discuss your feelings with him. Help protect him by not exposing him to some women. You are not expected to volunteer his services as a taxi driver. It is not smart to encourage him to take ladies home alone. Remind him of his professional responsibility to take precautions when counseling ladies. Some pastors feel invincible and do not admit the need for caution. Counseling should not take place in a solitary area. There ought to be another responsible person within a reasonable distance of the counseling site. There are certain precautions that all counselors should observe, and pastors are not the exception.

Always remember that your husband needs to have his social, spiritual, and sexual needs satisfied. By filling his emotional tank, you are protecting your spouse from external attacks. During periods of professional frustration and domestic pressures, the pastor is extremely vulnerable. In their book *Pastors at Risk,* London and Wiseman make the following statement: "Pastors are alarmingly vulnerable to outside emotional support during seasons of frustrating futility. That is why every possible prevention component that flows from a fulfilled marriage must never be permitted to falter." (47)

Finally, pray with and for your husband. We want our families to succeed, but we cannot do it alone. Good intentions, skill, and experience are not enough for a successful family life. In the face of all of these challenges, we need help. Proverbs 3:6 gives us assurance: "Trust in the Lord with all your heart, and lean not on your own understanding. In all thy ways acknowledge Him, and He will direct your paths" (KJV). With God as your Helper, work together with your husband to preserve your marriage and your ministry.

Male Wolves

"Wolves" will attack anyone, even the pastor's wife. Therefore, she also needs to be on her guard for any potential danger. Careless, naïve behavior will not protect her. She must exercise discretion, propriety, and good common sense. Often a woman can sense a potential predator. Therefore, she needs to have a battle plan before the attack.

Lingering handshakes and suggestive looks are indicators of a lurking wolf. Limit any physical contact. It is not necessary to hug every male parishioner. The clergy wife needs to avoid close, frequent contact with certain types of men. It is a good idea to avoid the entertaining of "wolves" when the pastor is absent. Steer conversations away from themes like loneliness, self-pity, personal financial problems, or your marital challenges. These present a suitable climate for infidelity. Confiding in male parishioners is not recommended. If you feel the need to share a problem, look for a professional counselor.

Do not put yourself in the position to receive or accept gifts from men.

Gifts from males should be presented to the family and not be personally dedicated to the pastor's wife. Sometimes a woman becomes an innocent victim of this gesture.

All men are not wolves. Our families need the support and help of some of our male church members. We appreciate their willingness to share their skills with us. In our ministry, we have been blessed by the kindness of unselfish, caring men. These men have been always ready and willing to help our family with emergencies and crises that always seemed to occur when my husband was away on a trip. Thank God for honest, Christian men of integrity. Our church is proud of such wonderful men of God.

Some ladies are caught off guard because they are slow in recognizing wolves. I came across the following striking statement from an anonymous writer. " If you ever have the opportunity to look into the eyes of a wolf, you will realize you are not looking into the eyes of just any animal; this one is thinking, with an intelligence you are not used to seeing in any animal." It is important to study human nature and be perceptive. We need to use our God-given radar to alert us to situations that could be dangerous. The Bible urges us to be wise as serpents and harmless as doves. Jesus promises to show us the way and guide us. "For this God is our God for ever and ever; he will be our guide even to the death" (Ps. 48:14). All we need to do is follow Him.

Build your relationship with your husband. Communicate regularly with him. Recognize your vulnerability and hold on to Jesus in your private devotional life. Add some physical and mental activities to your devotional life. Exercise, get a hobby, and read. By fortifying your mind, you will be able to put a great distance between you and your temptations. Do not take risks, and never deny the possibility that you could become a victim of indiscretion or even infidelity. It is safer to think *I am vulnerable. It could happen to me, too.*

Ways to Prevent Infidelity

Some decades ago, it was the male spouse who was more often trapped by infidelity. As time went by, more women entered the job market and assumed more economic independence and social confidence, and infidelity crept into the ranks of females. Formerly, Satan entrapped male pastors into infidelity. He realized that that was an effective way to paralyze the man of God into ineffective witnessing. We notice that in recent times, the snare of entrapment has been extended to pastors' wives. No one is exempt from the threat of infidelity. Pastors' wives who have been caught in infidelity have offered various explanations for this misfortune: loneliness, boredom, the inability to live under constant scrutiny, lack of spousal attention and caring, over-work, disillusionment, and the compelling urge to become rebellious and to exit the ministry. Not one of these pastors' wives who were interviewed stated that they ever dreamed this would happen. They were all good women with noble aspirations to serve the Lord in team ministry. But the devil used every avenue he could find and was successful.

The following is a list of strategies to combat infidelity:

1. Do not be over confident. Never say, "It can never happen to me." The Scriptures say, "Wherefore let him that thinketh he standeth take heed lest he fall" (1 Cor. 10:12). Be alert. Vigilance is a faithful companion of women.

2. Have strong moral convictions. Remember your values and refuse to compromise with sin. Rationalization is dangerous.

3. Be best friends with your spouse. Many occurrences of infidelity began with the "just friends" approach in a relationship. Make your spouse your best friend.

4. Set limits. Remember whose child you are. You are a child of the King of heaven. Royalty has standards of correct behavior. It is not necessary to be popular, but it is mandatory to be virtuous.

5. Build your own marriage. A successful marriage is the result of hard work. Entrust your marriage to God and do all that is humanly possible to make it work.

6. Accept responsibility for your behavior. You are a knowledgeable adult, and you are aware of Christian standards. Do not blame your behavior on circumstances.

7. Transform your thoughts. The apostle Paul shares the secret of elevating our thoughts: "Whatsoever things are pure . . . think on these things" (Phil. 4:8, NIV).

8. Pray, pray, pray. The habit of continuous prayer is necessary for our spiritual success. Paul admonishes us to "pray without ceasing" (1 Thess.

5:17); this should be our motto. This will keep Christ in our hearts.

9. Run if you have to. It is not only the coward who runs away. Wise men are brave enough to run from sinful, dangerous situations. Joseph's integrity propelled him away from Potiphar's wife, who tried to seduce him. He was determined not to "do this great wickedness and sin against God. . . . And he left his garment in her hand, and fled, and got him out" (Gen. 39:1-12 KJV).

The Three Little Pigs

Many of us have read the story entitled "The Three Little Pigs." One version of the story states that three pigs, Peter, Patty, and Penny, each decided to build a house. Peter built his house of straw, Patty built a wooden house, and Penny built her house of bricks.

Along came a wolf. He knocked on Peter's house of straw, demanding to be let in. Peter refused, and the big bad wolf threatened, "I'll huff and I'll puff and I'll blow your house in." This he did, and he destroyed Peter's house. The wolf then went to Patty's wooden house and did the same thing because Patty would not let him in.

Both Peter and Patty ran to Penny's brick house and warned her of the dangerous wolf. Along came the wolf, who tried to get in. "I'll huff and I'll puff and I'll blow your house in," thundered the bad wolf. But this time, he didn't succeed. The three little pigs united their efforts and defeated the big bad wolf.

Satan is the big bad wolf who is determined to destroy our homes. He targets pastoral families. He especially wants to "blow our house in." We have to build our house on the Rock, Jesus.

It Is Possible

You can have a successful pastoral marriage. It requires hard work and the determination to make the marriage work. London and Wiseman make the following comment: "To enjoy a high-octane marriage, two pressing inner issues need constant tending by the pastor and his wife: spiritual reality and emotional nourishment. Effective ministry cannot be done by either partner without these elements in abundant supply. . . . Create a caring environment where you both nourish spiritual reality and emotional strength in the other." (92)

The good news is that God is on our side. Our heavenly Father is committed to sustaining us and promoting happy and successful marriages. Above all, He is "able to keep you from falling" (Jude 24). Let us claim that precious promise for survival, enjoyment, and fulfillment in our lives.

CHAPTER 14

TAKING CARE OF YOURSELF

Often we tend to think that our bodies will take care of themselves. Perhaps it is because we are lucky enough to stay fit in spite of our carelessness—sometimes. We feed our husbands and children and omit setting a place at the table for ourselves. We carefully keep our children's immunization appointments but skip our mammograms. And that's not all. We postpone going to the beauty parlor but promptly send our sons to the barber so that they look smart all the time. We insist that our toddlers take their daily naps and observe strict bedtimes for our children, but we exhaust ourselves by working 'round the clock. We replace our children's clothes when they have outgrown them but are reluctant to upgrade our own wardrobes. We contribute to the fresh, crisp look of our husbands but pay less attention to our own appearance.

Take a Look at Ourselves

We need to commit ourselves to taking care of our general appearance and our health. The psalmist declares that we are "fearfully and wonderfully made." What a blessing! Yet sometimes we forget how precious we are, and we abuse or neglect ourselves. The other day I noted that the busy, virtuous woman of Proverbs 31 had some balance in her life. Despite her whirlwind of activities, she "maketh herself coverings of tapestry; her clothing is silk and purple" (Prov. 31:22). In his book *Exploring Proverbs,* John Phillips refers to the attractiveness of the Proverbs 31 woman: "Her devoted husband liked her to dress well. She had earned the right to wear silk and purple. She was a queen in her own right. . . . The ideal woman wore her fine clothes with an unconscious grace and a total lack of ostentatious pride." (601)

In Chapter Seven we talked a bit about the importance of our appearance. Since we are considering taking care of ourselves as a total package, it is necessary to revisit this theme. In many seminars, pastors' wives often reopen discussions on dress and appearance. Parishioners also comment on how the pastor's wife looks. Care of ourselves includes taking care of our appearance.

We need not seek to drape ourselves in ultra-expensive threads, but we must wear the best we can afford! Fabric, style, and fit must combine to bring out the "queen" in us. This is not an attempt to throw economy and frugality to the wind. If we look carefully in the stores, we may be fortunate enough to find bargains that are tasteful and becoming. Whenever I enter a store, I head straight for the sales rack. I am convinced that a bargain does not need to look like a bargain. Only our pocketbooks need to share that secret with us! I am always thrilled when I discover a very expensive dress that has been reduced to seventy percent off the original price. I grab it and walk out of that store feeling like a winner. Then when I wear the dress, I feel expensive and pretty. Ladies who sew have a greater advantage. They can pick styles that suit them and exercise their creativity to make themselves look beautiful at a lower cost. In all of this, we must always remember that modesty and appropriateness should be our guidelines when we dress ourselves.

How Can I Tell What is Right for Me?

I like the words of Carole Jackson in *Color Me Beautiful:*"Fashion is only as good as it looks on you. Some women seem to be able to wear the latest lines every year, but most of us cannot. The smart woman adapts the latest look to her own figure and personality rather than trying to alter her personal look to accommodate each trend. If you wear a style that doesn't look good on you—even if it's "in"—you do not look stylish." (94)

Shape, age, personality, and our position or profession should advise our choice of clothes. Add to this our complexion, the shape of our faces, our height, the length of our necks and hair, and of course a commitment to our Christian witness. This means that we really have to know ourselves. What kind of person am I? Am I outgoing? Am I reserved? Do I like bright colors or do I prefer milder colors? When I step into a store, can I tell if an outfit looks like me? How comfortable am I with my choice, in spite of the wooing of the sales attendant? If we are not sure what is good for us, it is all right for us to talk with someone who is an expert. Avoid the pitfall of being influenced to wear styles that do not reflect Christian standards. A Christian woman who is beautifully packaged can make an unbelievably stunning statement.

True Beauty is Deeper

I had a disappointing experience some time ago. A young lady came into a department store looking picture-perfect. She moved with confidence, and her dress and accessories were obviously chosen with care. A pair of bright, alert eyes was set in her youthful face. She seemed to have stepped right out of a catalog. One could not help but admire her. I found myself thinking of the many opportunities that probably lay ahead of this young lady. Then it happened. She placed her small purchase on the counter, but the cashier rang up the wrong price on the register. What an explosion of insults tumbled out of the young lady's well-made-up lips! Suddenly this beauty was transformed into a monster! A worn and faded rag doll would have had more appeal. Physical appearance is not beauty; but a mere outer layer. True beauty is also comprised of grace, refinement, patience, tolerance, and other "fruits of the spirit: love, joy, peace, longsuffering, gentleness, meekness, goodness, faith." (Gal. 4:22)

What About Our Health?

No one has to tell us how important it is to take care of our health. The point is that while we are aware of this, we claim that we are often *too busy*. There are so many things that can go wrong in a woman's body. We need to take the time to check on ourselves. There are some things that are helpful when we go to the doctor. According to *Health Hints for Women*, women should remember these essentials when visiting the doctor:

- *A clothes-on consultation.* This isn't always standard procedure, yet it is intimidating and distracting to talk to your doctor while sitting exposed and vulnerable in a drafty room.
- *A review of your list.* A study at the University of Dayton in Ohio found that patients who wrote down a list of questions to ask their doctors left their appointments feeling less anxious than those who didn't.
- *A Pap test, and of course the lowdown on the lab.* Scary reports surface from time to time about the quality of labs that analyze Pap tests.
- *Test results.* Request that a copy of the lab report be mailed to you; you

can verify your name and Social Security number to rule out mix-ups. (130-132)

These are just a few reminders and tips. A regular breast examination and an annual mammogram are strongly recommended for women. In fact, it is a good idea to examine one's own breasts once a month. Your regular visit to a doctor is needed as well. This will often aid in early detection of breast cancer.

Many women find mammograms uncomfortable. Here is a humorous account about one's preparation for a mammogram:

Suggested Breast Preparations for a Mammogram

If you think your breast may be in less than top form, prepare for a mammogram using these simple exercises:

Exercise 1: Refrigerate two bookends overnight. Lay one of your breasts (either will do) between the two bookends and smash the bookends together as hard you can. Repeat three times daily, more if possible.

Exercise 2: Locate a pasta maker or old wringer washer. Feed the breast into the machine and start cranking. Repeat twice daily.

Exercise 3 (Advanced Breast Preparation): Situate yourself comfortably as you lay on your side on the garage floor. Place one of your breasts snugly behind the rear tire of the family van. When you give the signal, hubby (or other Breast Preparer Buddy) will slowly ease the car into reverse. Hold for five seconds. Repeat on the other side.

Exercises 1 and 2 should be done frequently during the entire life of your breast; however, Exercise 3 should be only done one time per week for the four weeks prior to an actual mammogram procedure.

Please note, these are only suggested preparations. As in childbirth, nothing can truly prepare you for the real experience! (Contributed to *Swenny's E-mail Funnies* by Kathy Lydon, Chicago, Illinois).

As you take your health seriously, read as much as you can on various aspects of women's health. Our health is priceless, so we must resolve to take good care of it. The results will be fantastic, and our happiness will be increased. God will be pleased by our efforts. Instead of taking our bodies for granted, let our theme be, "I will praise You, for I am fearfully and wonderfully made; marvelous are Your works, and that my soul knows very well" (Ps. 139:14).

Accepting Care from Others

Who takes care of the caregiver? As clergy wives, we constantly make ourselves available to people who need our help. People's challenges become our problems. People's pain brings tears to our eyes. The heartache of a parishioner starts a stabbing sensation in our chests. We are there for them all.

Then comes our turn to cope with adversity. Our "ideal" pastoral family is threatened. Perhaps our dwindling finances force us into sleepless nights. There may be spousal disunity in the home. A sudden and serious illness (which the pastoral couple is not ready to disclose to the congregation) may strike. There is the combination of a burned-out, misunderstood husband and a confused, disillusioned wife. The ministerial couple becomes intolerant of each other, and the children are uncomfortable and scared of the future. Things seem to be falling apart. Where can we get help? We question why we should even appear helpless. We have all of the necessary resources and training. We dare not ask for help. Right? No, wrong.

"One of the most humbling but liberating experiences in life is to ask for help in areas where we think we should be competent," comments Sheila Walsh in *I'm Not Wonder Woman but God Made Me Wonderful!* (134) Make no mistake. It is neither a sin nor a sign of weakness to ask for help. The difficulty lies in finding the right person from whom we can get help. We are often caught between disclosing and concealing our weaknesses or pain. We are afraid of appearing vulnerable. We prefer to hide our struggles from the church members. We hold on to our professional poise and continue to flash our plastic smiles. Yet the anguish in our hearts devours our happiness and erodes our family relationships.

It is at this time that we need to look for professional help. Someone who is a Christian counselor could be of great assistance. If you do not know of a Christian counselor in your area, you may be able to find a listing of Christian counselors online or at the local library. There are also counseling centers for ministry couples. Perhaps you may even need to go to a nearby town to meet with a counselor. The point is not to bear your burdens alone. God has provided skilled practitioners to help you.

It is easy to question our right to be in the ministry when challenges oppress us. Why should people who are called by God need counseling? We may be tempted to believe that a truly consecrated ministerial worker has no need of a psychiatrist. If there is such a need, the minister and his wife are not authentic. These are erroneous judgments. In fact, this outlook is designed to wreak further havoc in the life of a minister and his family. We do not need an excuse to seek help. We need only the cause and symptoms. If we broke a leg or damaged an eye, we would not struggle for a rationale to rush to a physician, would we? In the same way, when we have emotional pain or family challenges, we need to go for help, quickly. The sooner we recognize our humanity, the easier it is for us to seek professional help in our times of need. Edward B Bratcher supports the need for help for the minister's wife: "I believe that the minister's wife is in need of help. This applies to all—minister, spouse, and children. Because the divorce rate among clergy is well below the national average, a false impression that all is well with the families of the clergy has developed. And even with the increase of divorce among the clergy, there still seems to be a belief that clergy marriages are less vulnerable to problems. This is not true. Ministry is a strain even on a strong marriage." (84)

Why Care is Necessary

It is accepted that the ministry abounds in challenges. Louis McBurney throws clarity on this:

> "Pressures in the ministry aren't new. Paul was obviously aware of the difficulties when he recommended a life of celibacy because of the demands of the ministry. It may be that the intensity of the problems has not changed since. The loss of privacy, the poor pay, the unrealistic expectations and the frustrations inherent in church work have long been identified. . . . However, there are other indications that life in the ministry may be increasingly difficult. The community respect that clergy once commanded has been eroded . . . another changing statistic is the number of clergy divorces. There has been a marked rise in the number of clergy marriages ending in divorce in the last ten to fifteen years." (24, 25)

When the problems are heavy and there seems to be a dire need for help, get help—medical or psychological. There is no disgrace in seeking professional help. When you do not feel well or when your body or mind feel different, get help. Perhaps you suffer loss of appetite or sleep. Perhaps you want to be isolated. You may be irritable or lethargic. There may be definite physical symptoms. If you have persistent feelings of being unwell, get help quickly. The first step is to see a physician who will be able to give you guidance and direct you.

God wants us to be healthy and happy. "Beloved, I pray that you may prosper in all things and be in health, just as your soul prospers (3 John 2, NKJV).

CHAPTER 15

WHAT SHALL WE DO TODAY?

There is no lack of engagements or activities for the pastor's wife. She is a very busy lady! However, sometimes we wonder what is God purpose for our lives. There are times when God's purpose for our lives seems obvious. At other times we wish for a clear sign from heaven.

God is willing to give us wisdom and guidance. God has promised that if you sincerely seek God's guidance, He will give it. The Bible contains several assurances of God's guidance in the lives of His people.

Many of us serve willingly in our churches, and this is good. As servants of God, though, we ought not to confine our blessings to a limited area. Our commitment to service should extend beyond the walls of our churches and into our communities. This is not a suggestion to overburden ourselves; but merely an "awareness call" to sensitize us to the needs of a dying world.

Many of our churches are blessed with numerous talented people who minister. Our service in the church adds to the pool of blessings there. However, it is commendable to pour some of these blessings into the community.

Does Charity Remain at Home?

Picture a wealthy family having a large feast. There is an abundance of food on the table. There are so many wonderful items to choose from! The specially invited guests almost gorge themselves with the delicacies. The hostess invites guests to eat more and more, but this is impossible. The guests have reached their limits. Trays and trays of untouched food are left.

Just outside the gates of the banquet house are scores of hungry children. Some hungry, homeless people roam the streets desperately seeking a morsel. For them, food seems elusive. Meanwhile, at the banquet house, the hostess decides to pack the unused food into take-out boxes and present it to the already overfilled guests. The many hungry mouths remain outside the gates.

Perhaps the hostess does not know of the hungry people outside in the cold streets. Perhaps this is the first day that hungry, homeless people chose to go on that street. Maybe the hostess fears that an initial show of generosity will encourage the indigent to habitually beat a path to her affluent house. What would her wealthy neighbors think? They would probably be offended. Whatever the reason, the fact remains that the people in the street are starving.

Some pastors' wives complain that their services are neither sought nor appreciated by their church. Perhaps there is a glut of talent in the church. Of course one can find or even create an area of service. It is not necessary to serve in the conventional areas only. When God reveals a need to us, we must serve.

Shining in Our Community

There are many things we can do to share our love and blessings with the community. One does not have to undertake mammoth projects; just a little thoughtfulness here and there can be a marvelous ministry.

One of the popular methods is to carry a tract or inspirational book or card in our handbags and give them to random persons. Pray before you leave your house, and God will show you a person in need of a blessing.

Discuss some community projects with other pastors' wives and assign yourselves different tasks. Divide the projects according to groups in the community: the elderly, teenage mothers, the disabled, the homeless, orphanages, rehabilitation centers. It is amazing how many people groups you can think of during a brainstorming session.

Make a list of ministry ideas and assign a project to each of the ministry wives. The tasks need not be labor-intensive or time-consuming. The objective is to shine a light, even a little candle, in your community.

Here is a starter list of possible projects:

- Distribute care packages to homeless shelters.
- Bake something simple and distribute it to a poor neighborhood.
- Take an elderly person on a trip to the mall or shopping center.
- Run an errand for someone.
- Gift-wrap some devotional books and give them to everyone you meet.

- Prepare some lunches and give them to the homeless on the streets.
- Go prayer-walking.
- Put health magazines in the waiting rooms at doctors' offices.
- Organize some young people from your church to paint a fence or cut the lawn for an elderly person.
- Take some parenting literature and make a care package for a teenage mother.

These projects are relatively simple. There are many more involved and time-consuming tasks that some people may want to do. The idea is to let our light shine in our communities.

It's All About Servanthood

We can serve in many ways. Regardless of our age or station in life, we can serve. Servanthood is the state of ministering happily to others. Those to whom we minister may or may not be in dire need, but our love for service and the desire to serve (that is inspired by Jesus within our hearts) will drive us to do this. Servanthood is not a yoke of subservience borne by one influenced by a slavish mentality. On the contrary, the woman who is confident that she is a child of God will serve gladly. This is because she possesses supreme self-worth.

Servanthood is the handmaid of humility. Humility is freedom from pride, arrogance, and conceit. While aware of her virtues, talents, and skills, the humble woman will see herself as possessing weaknesses, "righteousness as filthy rags." She will recognize her need for the grace of Jesus to make her all she should be. Having embraced this grace, she will celebrate this wonderful gift by serving others.

Our Lord Jesus was the example of servanthood. "Whoever wants to become great among you must be your servant . . . just as the Son of Man did not come to be served, but to serve" (Matt. 20:26-28).

Lord, show me opportunities for service. Then fill my heart with Your love that compels me to serve humanity.

CHAPTER 16

WHEN YOUR MARRIAGE IS IN TROUBLE

Being in a ministerial family does not guarantee immunity from family challenges. All kinds of problems stalk God's people. Families are under constant attack from Satan.

Claudette and Ken (not their real names) had been married for six years. Ken was working with a large congregation in the city. Claudette was an elementary school teacher. They had no children as yet. Claudette and Ken were not happy. Often they snapped at each other. Their words were fierce, and sometimes Claudette feared that Ken came close to hitting her. Where had the love and romance gone? When did the deterioration all begin?

Ken began to dread going home after work because he and Claudette always had an argument. He knew that there would be no meal awaiting him; in fact, there was no official mealtime anymore. The house was slowly becoming a tomb. This seemed to be a dying marriage. Claudette found herself detesting the very sight of Ken.

Failing ministerial marriages are very common these days. Every trace of selfishness, every indication of cruelty, every manifestation of insensitivity, every display of violence, every show of intolerance, the refusal to meet one another's needs—everything that threatens domestic harmony is a mode of satanic intervention. This realization would help us to be guarded and to align ourselves with the forces of heaven. It is also important to agree on a strategy for handling unfavorable domestic situations before times of real conflict and crisis occur.

When initial hints of marital trouble present themselves, this is the time to pay attention to the situation. Little disagreements increase in size and intensity. We need to take seriously the little irritations that have the potential for monstrous growth. Identify problems. Admit that they exist. Sometimes we prefer to believe that we do not have problems. Why should a clergy family admit that their marriage is in trouble? And if there is impending trouble, why should we seek help? We are the experts. Besides, we do not want the parishioners to know about our challenges. (Very often they already know). The wise man, Solomon advises us to start early when problems arise: "Catch for us the foxes, the little foxes that ruin the vineyards, our vineyards that are in bloom" (Song of Solomon 2:15, NIV). Too often we wait until the "foxes" have grown to unmanageable proportions before we try to deal with them. Little problems left unattended will increase exponentially in magnitude.

Why Some Ministerial Marriages Fail

Many circumstances can lead to marital difficulty in ministerial families. Stress in the ministerial family is one factor that can result in bickering and unpleasantness. Overwork and fatigue can cause intolerance and emotional outbursts. The ministerial wife is sometimes disenchanted because she does not find the joy she had hoped to find in ministry. Financial challenges can also weigh heavily on the family. Prolonged illness is another threat to marital happiness. Children who are becoming rebellious are a strain on their parents. Pressure from administrators coupled with the demands and criticism of church members are an additional cause. Any one of these or a combination of factors can provide fertile ground for marital disharmony. The difference between failing marriages and successful marriages is not the absence of difficulties; the difference lies in the ability of the couple to say, "We have a problem, let us work it out."

Communication Again

Communicating our problems with each other is always helpful. Almost every aspect of marital discord can be linked to faulty communication. Keeping silent about our pain and fears causes damage to any relationship. When family members refuse to share their needs and hurts, there is a build-up of resentment. Anger, disillusionment, and emotional distance follow. Communication involves listening, speaking, sharing different levels of feelings, and seeking to understand one another. The Word of God contains sound principles of communication in Proverbs 15–18 and James 1:19. Study a few of these principles daily. Communication is a skill that needs to be practiced. It is a difficult art, but also a critical ingredient of success.

Be prepared to work for the success of your marriage. Good marriages do not just happen. The following statement from *The Adventist Home* is very striking: "To gain a proper understanding of the marriage relation is the work of a lifetime.... However carefully and wisely marriage may have been entered into, few couples are completely united when the marriage ceremony is performed. The real union of the two in wedlock is the work of after years" (Ellen G. White, 105).

As in every other aspect of life, seek God's help. He has promised wisdom and assistance. Do not have unrealistic expectations of each other. Remember that we are all vulnerable to Satan's attacks. Patience, love, understanding, and the spirit of forgiveness are helpful in maintaining a marriage.

The sense of binding commitment will cement your relationship. Reaffirm your commitment to God and to each other. Banish any thought of having chosen the wrong partner. You are together already. Guard your investment of time and energy. Every day that you have been married is an investment of your time in the marriage. No one wants to throw away an investment in which so much has been given. Anything that can be done to salvage it is worth trying.

Professional Help Needed

If your own efforts prove futile, do not hesitate to seek help. It is a blessing to be able to go to a counselor in an effort to save the marriage. One of the benefits of professional assistance is that the couple gets the opportunity to disclose their pain, observations, and general feelings in a safe environment free from the attacks of each spouse.

Another point in favor of a visit to a professional is that professionals are expected to be confidential. The fear that the internal struggles and resentments of the clergy family will be exposed could be eliminated here.

One can gain greater insight into causes of certain behaviors. Analyses and assessments are done that direct the sessions of therapy. Sometimes personality and temperament tests are administered. These prove to be not only revealing but also very helpful. The clients therefore learn more about themselves and their spouses.

Christian counselors offer hope, and their resources are enriched because they are aided by Christ, the "wonderful Counselor." Apart from the therapy received from professionals, there are many books and CDs that are valuable aids to successful family living. Invest in a library of resources for the family.

Do not underestimate the power of professional help. Disregard the temptation to try to heal your own situation if things seem to be getting out of control. This is not necessary. God has placed several gifts in His church. Sometimes we need to accept help. What do you do if the pastor cannot be convinced to seek help? Pray first about his reluctance. Then let your husband know that your marriage and family are of such tremendous importance to you that you would like both of you to seek help. Resist the urge to point fingers of blame at each other. Perhaps you may even want to admit to your own contribution to the problem. Keep your objective in full view. You are trying to convince your spouse that it is crucial for both of you to secure help. Use your feminine skills to achieve success in this.

Sharing Your Troubles

It is difficult to bear our burdens alone for a considerable amount of time. The heart needs some release. Oh yes, we talk to God, but we often need to do some venting to someone else. Resist the temptation. Do not discuss the details of your marital disappointments with others except in a professional capacity. That is why a therapist is needed. Many people are curious to discover what goes on in pastoral households. This is not to be revealed to them. The "sacred circle" must be preserved. Share your troubles with a professional. There have been many painful experiences that resulted from a heavy-hearted sister and brother baring their souls to gossip vendors. Since we do not know the hearts of persons, we can never be too careful.

Leave or Cleave?

A young clergy wife told me the other day that she had had enough of the manse. She was going to leave! She and her husband had two kids, and she was going to take the kids and leave. She did not even want to be near her husband. Her pain had increased and so had her hatred and anger. This ministerial couple had not spoken to each other for some time. The kids were confused and unhappy, their grades in school dropped, and they became discipline problems. Fortunately, this couple hurried into a counseling program. Although they had "hated" each other, they were prepared to pursue restoration. Their relationship was repaired. That marriage was saved.

Other stories have had tragic endings. The partners were adamant about their decision to separate and even got divorced. Some changed careers. Their children were devastated. Parishioners were crushed. Friends and colleagues were hurt. Heaven mourned, and the devil scored another victory.

It is important to realize that divorce is not inevitable. Successful marriages still exist. Often divorce as a solution for marriage problems is worse than the disease it was intended to cure. Numerous studies on the impact of divorce on the parties involved clearly show that divorce is never "successful." It is one of the biggest tragedies that a person can experience. The impact on the ex-wife, ex-husband, and on the children is nothing short of disastrous. It is like a nightmare from which most never awake. It is no wonder that God says, "I hate divorce" (Mal. 2:16, NIV).

Cling to the hope that your marriage can be mended. Your marriage is worth all the effort it demands to preserve it. Know that you have all the resources of heaven on your side. God can help you in your struggles. He is the Creator of marriage and the family. Trust Him to guide you and keep you. He will never fail you.

CHAPTER 17

HE'S ABLE

As we ponder the responsibilities of a pastor's wife, we wonder, *Who is able to cope with all of these things?* What full plates we carry! Several years ago there was a popular television commercial for a dishwashing liquid. The commercial showed a young woman, obviously overwhelmed. There were dishes everywhere. The kitchen sink overflowed with dishes. Some dishes had even been tucked into the oven so that they could be concealed from full view. The kitchen table and counters were strewn with dishes. In a corner of the kitchen floor, were stacks of pots and pans. Dishes, dirty dishes, were everywhere. As the young woman sat on the kitchen floor surveying this domestic chaos, a voice verbalized her feelings, "What's a girl like you doing in a place like this?"

Having a Party?

How often have we not felt like the young woman in the television commercial! As the demands of the parish seem to drown us, we doubt our ability to surface and survive. It is difficult not to feel overwhelmed. Our feelings of despair manifest themselves in various ways. We may become grumpy and irritable in our homes. That means that our loved ones get the brunt of our unpleasantness. Oh, we are able to muster a few scant sweet smiles for the people at church or in the community, but at home we release our harsh words and exhibit intolerance. In the midst of her turmoil, one wife told her children, "I am going to run away!" The poor lady meant it. She was overcome with stress.

We may decide to host or join a pity party at which we sit and feel sorry for ourselves. This is very easy to do when we are frustrated or burned out. We tally the number of expectations people have of us. Then we add the list of spoken or unspoken expectations from our spouses. We reminisce about the days of our youth when we were free, single, and "normal." By this time, the items on the menu at our "party" increase. There is much for us to feast on.

Satan, who is the real host of our pity party, holds a shimmering tray inviting us to partake of his "niceties." There is a tossed salad of disappointment and disillusionment. Large tumblers of our unmet needs meet our inward gaze. There is a large serving of our memories of criticism. In addition, there is a generous slice of resentment garnished with bitterness toward our ever-busy, often absentee husbands. We fill our aching stomachs with accumulated hurts. Some of us help ourselves to second and even third servings. The party is in full swing.

Then Satan turns up the music. It deafens our consciences. The drums of regret, self-pity, and even anger beat louder. Satan blows his trumpets of rebellion in our ears. "You do not have to bear this. Ministry is unrewarding and unthankful," he reinforces. "There isn't even money in it. Your children are draining your resources. Your husband is hardly at home to help you. All you do is give, give, give. Why not give up now? Forget about 'the call.' How do you know you were cut out for this minister's wife thing anyway? It's time to discard that 'first lady' garb. Just think of how cool it would be to be able to be yourself. Isn't this what you have wanted for a long time? Go for it."

The music gets louder. Satan comes closer. "Shall we dance?" comes his fiendish invitation. He waltzes closer and closer to you. There is a heat in the room. Your head spins as you process your feelings and the pressure. You are tempted to give in and give up.

It is Satan's plan to weigh us down with despair. He presents himself when we are most vulnerable. He is adept at this. There is really no easy way out with the devil. Yet he tries to convince us to accept him. He even tried this scheme with our Lord Jesus. Thank God, Jesus defeated Satan. That is why we can succeed through the strength and victory in Jesus.

Circumstances may overwhelm us. The pressures of life may reduce our vital force, but by God's grace we can emerge victorious. This will be possible as we lean on Jesus. We dare not rely on our own resources. God has promised to sustain and support us. "The Lord is my strength and song, and He has become my salvation" (Exod. 15:2, NASB).

The Party Is Over

When we feel debilitated and faint, the power of God's love will bear us up. In moments of greatest weakness, we can throw ourselves into the arms of our loving Lord who has promised, "My grace is sufficient for you, for my strength is made perfect in weakness" (2 Cor. 12:9, NKJV).

We may feel *down* sometimes, but thank God we will not be *out*. In times like these, it helps to stop and count our blessings. There are so many things that we tend to take for granted. Make a list of common blessings and remember unique blessings too. Count your blessings, linger over your list, and feel your tension melt.

God holds His divine arms beneath us like a giant safety net. "The eternal God is thy refuge, and underneath are the everlasting arms" (Deut. 33:27). When we feel desperate, we can run and even jump into the arms of God.

He's Always Able

We may stumble beneath the load of challenges. Even when our footsteps falter, we do not have to fall. We cannot fall while we keep our hands in the hands of Jesus. Allow Him to hold you, to hug you, to bless you. God can and will do it for you. All we need to do is ask Him. He is "able to do exceeding abundantly above all that we can ask or think" (Eph. 3:20). Consider this string of superlatives: "exceeding, abundantly, above all." Our God is not a minimum-wage god. Our God has limitless resources. Our God is abundant. Praise His name!

We are not promised a thimbleful of strength. We are promised *His* strength and His grace. We can make it. We need not fall. Why? Jesus has promised to sustain us to the end. You are special to God. God has great plans for you. Jesus wants to present you with pride to His Father as a champion. That is why He has promised to keep us from falling.

Claim His promise. And guess what? He can do it. "To him who is able to keep you from falling and to present you before his glorious presence, without fault and with great joy—to the only God our Savior be glory, majesty, power and authority, through Jesus Christ our Lord, before all ages, now and forevermore!" (Jude 24, 25 NIV).

WORKS CITED

Alcorn, Randy and Nanci, *Women Under Stress: Preserving Your Sanity* (Portland: Oregon: Multnomah, 1986).

American Heritage Dictionary of the English Language, 4ᵗʰ ed. (USA: Houghton Mifflin, 2006).

Auerbach, Stephen M. and Sandra E. Grambling, *Stress Management: Psychological Foundations* (New Jersey: Prentice-Hall, 1998).

Baer, Greg, *Real Love in Marriage* (New York: Penguin Group, 2006).

Barnes, Emilie, *Survival for Busy Women* (Eugene, Oregon: Harvest House, 1993).

____, *Emilie's Creative Home Organizer* (Eugene, Oregon: Harvest House, 1995).

Bratcher, Edward B., *The Walk-On-Water Syndrome: Dealing with Professional Hazards in the Ministry* (Waco, Texas: Word Books, 1984).

Clairmont, Patsy, *Normal Is Just a Setting on Your Dryer* (Colorado Springs, Colorado: Focus on the Family, 1993).

Cousins, Norman. *The Anatomy of an Illness as Perceived by the Patient* (New York: Norton & Company, 1979).

Cress, Sharon M., ed., *Seasoned with Laughter* (Silver Spring, MD; Ministerial Assn., 1999).

Cureton, Kenyn, "The Minister's Shooting: Why Did She Kill Him?" *People,* March 31, 2006.

Davidson, Jeff, *The Complete Idiot's Guide to Managing Stress* (New York: Simon and Schuster, 1997).

Detweiler, M., assoc. ed., *Laughter for a Woman's Soul* (Grand Rapids, Michigan: Inspirio, 2001).

Dictionary.com Unabridged, based on *Random House's Unabridged Dictionary* (Random House, 2006).

Ducan, Lynne, ed. *Heart to Heart with Pastors' Wives* (Ventura, California: Regal, 1994).

Eppinger, Paul and Sybil, *Every Minister Needs a Lover* (Grand Rapids, Michigan:Baker Book House, 1990).

Felton, Sandra. *Smart Organizing: Simple Strategies for Bringing Order to Your Home* (Grand Rapids, Michigan: Fleming H. Revell, 2005).

_____, *Smart Organizer: Simple Strategies for Bringing Order to Your Home* (Grand Rapids, Michigan: Fleming H. Revell, 2001).

Harley, Willard F., Jr., *His Needs, Her Needs: Building An Affair-Proof Marriage* (Grand Rapids, Michigan: Fleming H. Revell, 2001).

Harrar, Sari, ed., *Health Hints for Women* (Emmaus, Pennsylvania: Rodale Press, 1997).

Jackson, Carole, *Color Me Beautiful* (New York: Ballantine Books, 1985).

Jeremiah, David, *Captured by Grace* (Nashville, Tennessee: Integrity Publishers, 2006).

Littauer, Florence, *Taking Charge of Your Life* (Grand Rapids, Michigan: Fleming H. Revell, 1999).

London, H. B. Jr. and Neil B. Wiseman, *Pastors at Greater Risk* (Ventura, California: Regal Books, 2003).

_____, *Pastors At Risk* (USA: Victor Books, 1993).

Lotz, Anne Graham, *My Heart's Cry* (Nashville, Tennessee: W Publishing, 2002).

McBurney, Louis, *Counseling Christian Workers* (Waco, Texas: Word Books, 1986).

Parrott, Leslie, *You Matter More Than You Think* (Grand Rapids, Michgan: Zondervan, 2006).

Patterson, Dorothy Kelley, *A Handbook for Ministers' Wives* (Nashville, Tennessee: Broadman & Holman, 2001).

Patton, Beth Ann, ed., *Laughter is the Spice of Life* (Nashville, Tennessee: W Publishing Group, 2004).

Phillips, John. *Exploring Proverbs,* vol. 2 (Neptune, New Jersey: Loizeaux Brothers, 1996).

Pines, Ayala M. *Keeping the Spark Alive: Preventing Burnout in Love and Marriage* (New York: St. Martin's, 1988).

Somerville, Mary, *One With a Shepherd: The Tears and Triumphs of a Ministry Marriage* (The Woodlands, Texas: Kress Christian Publications, 2005).

Taylor, Alice B., *How to Be a Minister's Wife and Love It* (Grand Rapids, Michigan: Zondervan, 1968).

Van Pelt, Nancy, *Creative Hospitality: How to Turn Home Entertaining into a Real Ministry* (Hagerstown, Maryland: Review and Herald Pub. Assn., 1998).

Walsh, Sheila, *I'm Not Wonder Woman but God Made Me Wonderful!* (Nashville, Tennessee: Thomas Nelson Inc., 2005).

White, Ellen G., *Education* (Nampa, Idaho: Pacific Press Pub. Assn., 1952).

____, *Messages to Young People* (Nashville, Tennessee: Southern Pub. Assn., 1930).

____, *Testimonies for the Church,* vol. 5. (Mountain View, California: Pacific Press Pub. Assn., 1948).

____, *Testimonies for the Church,* vol. 7 (Mountain View, California: Pacific Press Pub. Assn., 1948).

____, *The Adventist Home* (Nashville, Tennessee: Southern Pub. Assn., 1952).